Industrial and Organizational Psychology Supplement for Introductory Psychology

Sherri Lind Hughes, Ph. D.

Western Maryland College

HarperCollins*CollegePublishers*

Hughes INDUSTRIAL AND ORGANIZATIONAL PSYCHOLOGY
SUPPLEMENT FOR INTRODUCTORY PSYCHOLOGY

Copyright © 1994 HarperCollins College Publishers

ISBN: 0-673-99317-5

93 94 95 96 97 9 8 7 6 5 4 3 2 1

Table of Contents

Industrial and Organizational Psychology Supplement for Introductory Psychology

What is Industrial and Organizational Psychology?

Why Study Industrial and Organizational Psychology?

Many American citizens between the ages of 18 and 70 spend more than 40 hours per week in paid employment. Some are satisfied with their jobs and others are dissatisfied. Some are very productive and efficient at what they do and others are less so. What makes the difference? How do people choose the work they do, the organizations that they work for, and what they want from their jobs? Your answers to these questions may focus on wages or salary, how people are compensated for the work that they do. You may also think about personality, interests, or abilities: what people like or what they do well. Many other factors affect how well employees perform their jobs and how they fell about them including relationships with co-workers, safety and comfort of physical work environments, effectiveness of supervision and management, and the importance of the work itself.

In order to answer these and other questions, industrial and organizational psychologists study workers and the workplace. They use psychological methods and apply psychological principles to workplace problems. They are interested in achieving the best and most humane use of human resources for the employer and in creating an optimal work environment for the employees. While wages are an important issue in work satisfaction and productivity, there are many other important factors that determine whether employees and employers are effective in reaching their individual and organizational goals. Industrial and organizational psychologists are interested in identifying those factors and using their knowledge to create a more comfortable and more productive workplace.

What Do Industrial/Organizational Psychologists Do?

Most, if not all, working adults have felt the influence of industrial and organizational psychologists. As practitioners and researchers, I/O psychologists affect the ways in which people apply for a job and the ways in which they are interviewed or tested after they have applied. I/O psychologists develop training methods and programs that a new worker might encounter after he or she takes the job. Employees may occasionally be asked to complete a survey so that their employer has a better understanding of what they like and don't like about their work and working environment. An I/O psychologist might design the survey, analyze the results and recommend changes in policies or practices to the organization so that it has a mostly satisfied and perhaps more productive workforce.

In general, industrial and organizational psychologists study human work behavior and apply psychological knowledge, theories, and principles to enhance our understanding of workplace behavior and to improve the physical and social work environment. As a field, I/O psychology draws on resources and information from a variety of areas that you have already studied: **testing and psychometrics** for selecting employees and evaluating their work performance, **motivation** to enhance the productivity and efficiency of employees, **personality and social psychology** to understand the interactions between individuals and within groups, **learning** for training methods, and **cognitive psychology** to study decision making processes.   Overall, I/O psychologists are primarily interested in enhancing human work performance and improving the quality of employees' work lives. In addition, I/O psychologists address the important relationships between work and other components of an individual's life such as family, health, and leisure (Howard, 1991).

The field of industrial/organizational psychology is typically divided into two subfields: **industrial psychology** and **organizational psychology**. Industrial or personnel psychology emphasizes using psychological knowledge to understand and improve human resources within organizations. Psychologists in this area may focus on studying and implementing a fair selection system which allows an organization to choose the best person for a particular job by developing a good test. An industrial psychologist may also validate a structured interview to show that it will identify the best applicants for a job or evaluate the usefulness of a personality test for choosing managers. An industrial psychologist might conduct research to better understand the performance evaluation process: how is the job performance of employees assessed? Are the procedures used by the organization consistent across jobs and fair to all employees? Do these evaluations provide individuals with the feedback needed to improve performance? An industrial psychologist might also develop a training program for new workers and evaluate the usefulness of that program after it has been implemented. This effort would answer the question: Do the new employees learn what the organization needs for them to learn and can they use this knowledge on the job?

In contrast, organizational psychologists are more likely to focus on group processes and interactions within the workplace. An organizational psychologist might study the leadership styles of managers and identify which of those styles will best suit a particular work environment or job category. Is a leader directive, giving clear directions on what work to do and how to do it? Is a manager participative, asking subordinates for suggestions and encouraging them to give their opinions and make decisions? How do those behavior patterns influence subordinates? Organizational psychologists may also be interested in techniques that can be used to motivate employees to do their best work. Under what conditions are individuals motivated to fulfill their potential and maximize their performance? An organizational psychologist might also analyze the concepts of organizational climate and culture within a particular company. How do the individuals within the organization perceive the work environment and how does that affect their performance and attitudes about their work? Finally, organizational psychologists may study organizational development and implement organizational change, altering the structure and procedures within the organization to make it better able to fulfill its objectives by being more efficient, more productive, more creative, more flexible, or more safety conscious.

The History of Industrial and Organizational Psychology

Industrial and organizational psychology began to develop soon after the turn of the century. Most of the individuals in the field at this time had been trained as experimental psychologists but developed an interest in workplace issues when they were approached by employers to solve newly discovered problems in the workplace. For the most part individuals in the field at this time focused on selection, training, and job design to improve the efficiency of the work being done (Katzell & Austin, 1992). During World War I psychologists helped to develop a standardized system for selecting and placing military recruits. These efforts led to the development of two paper and pencil cognitive ability tests: Army Alpha and Army Beta (the latter was designed to test recruits who could not read or write). Psychologists working for the military also developed personality tests and measures of psychopathology to screen applicants for the military. After World War I the first consulting firms were organized in which groups of I/O psychologists provided services to a variety of organizations on a temporary or more limited basis. In addition, some I/O psychologists were employed full time in various industries such as insurance and retail.

4

During the 1930s some of the most famous studies within industrial and organizational psychology were conducted at Western Electric. The Hawthorne studies were designed to investigate how the work environment influences individual and group efficiency. Originally, these studies focused on the effects of working conditions such as lighting and noise, incentives, and fatigue on individual and group performance. Later, the researchers investigated the role of perceptions and attitudes in determining performance. The Hawthorne studies were one of the first attempts by I/O psychologists to study psychological phenomena in a realistic work environment. One of the most important outcomes from the Hawthorne studies was the recognition that how employees felt about their work and how they perceived the organization could substantially alter their job performance. After the Hawthorne studies, there was a growing interest in studying and measuring worker attitudes and job satisfaction. Psychologists and employers became interested in how employees felt about their work and how those attitudes might affect the quality and quantity of their work performance.

During World War II industrial/organizational psychologists again used their knowledge to help the war effort. During this time the Army General Classification Test (AGCT) was developed. This test was used to choose recruits and place them in the jobs for which they were best suited. It measured adult learning ability and aptitude for learning various occupations. Other I/O psychologists studied and developed training methods, team building techniques, and programs to enhance morale or change attitudes. After World War II, more organizations hired I/O psychologists to practice and conduct research and address their workplace concerns, and new consulting firms also got started. Organizational psychology became a more prominent part of the field with a new emphasis on studies of leadership, decision making processes, and motivational techniques. In addition, the prosperity of the postwar period allowed I/O psychologists and the organizations that employed them to become more concerned about the needs of employees rather than a strict emphasis on productivity and efficiency.

Since the 1960s, I/O psychologists have enlarged their knowledge base and improved the interventions that they design for the workplace. Pre-employment testing is continually improved, and new motivational techniques have been developed. I/O psychologists have studied how to design jobs so that they are interesting and motivating for workers and have introduced those job design models into the workplace. One of the major changes that has occurred within the field during this time is the introduction of civil rights legislation that prohibited discrimination in the workplace. These laws require I/O psychologists to evaluate the methods used to select and promote employees to ensure that they are not biased against individuals in various groups. These regulations have also prompted organizations to address the concerns about harmful employee and employer behaviors such as sexual harassment and racial discrimination. These efforts to maintain fair practices are ongoing as laws and regulations are reinterpreted in the courts and new legislation is passed.

Today I/O psychologists continue to use their knowledge about psychology to improve the work environment, to enhance productivity, and to address the concerns and needs of a more diverse workforce. Organizations must be able to promote the well-being of all of their employees including female, minority and disabled employees. They must also foster a sense of unity within a diverse workforce so that employees can work toward common organizational goals. Within the field of I/O psychology there is also an increasing interest in international organizational practices and understanding how culture affects the organization and its activities. I/O psychologists are also looking at a variety of issues concerning unemployment and retirement. What happens to individuals when they cannot work? How does it affect their psychological well-being and how does it affect those who remain with the same organization?

The Role of the Industrial/Organizational Psychologist

I/O psychologists can be employed in a variety of work settings. Typically an I/O psychologist will be employed in one of five job categories: private industry such as banks, manufacturers and telecommunications, academics including both business and psychology departments within major universities, four year colleges and community colleges, public organizations within federal, state, or local governments or the military, consulting firms which provide services for a variety of organizations, and self-employed as consultants (Howard, 1991). Figure 1 shows that most industrial and organizational psychologists work for private companies and consulting firms. Within these work settings I/O psychologists perform a number of different functions: they may conduct research to better understand organizational phenomena, or they may function as practitioners solving workplace problems. I/O psychologists may also be managers with responsibilities for supervising and developing a group of individuals who work for and with them. They may spend time teaching others about the field of I/O psychology or training people on a set of job skills. While I/O psychologists in academics conduct the most research and spend the most time on education, the independent consultants and those working for consulting firms spend the most time in practice (Howard, 1991).

The individuals in these work settings will necessarily have different interests and tasks to complete but also will have a number of common interests and activities. First, as a field, I/O psychology is founded in the **scientist/practitioner model**. This model suggests that I/O psychology is most effective when

7

**Figure 1
Work Settings of
industrial and organizational psychologists**

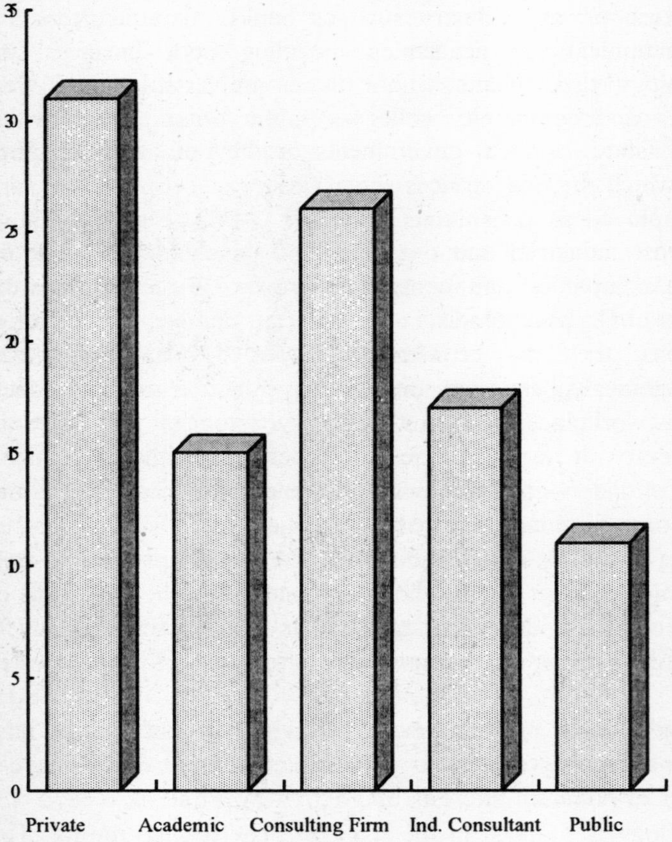

Private	
Academic	
Consulting Firm	
Ind. Consultant	
Public	

practice is based on scientific findings *and* when the research conducted draws its questions from practice within organizations. In their dual roles, I/O psychologists function as scientists conducting research to answer questions about the workplace and practitioners using those answers to solve workplace problems. For example, an I/O psychologist who has been asked to facilitate higher productivity in a plant manufacturing automobiles should conduct research on what factors motivate these individuals to perform well, factors such as wages, awards and recognition, day care or healthcare benefits, or the possibility of getting a promotion. Those results should be applied when developing the incentive program. Similarly, the research on human motivation should be designed to answer questions about how various incentive programs and other motivational techniques will affect performance in actual work environments.

These parallels may seem obvious but there is some concern within the field that I/O psychologists are moving away from the scientist/practitioner model because of the demands within their own work environments (Dunnette, 1990). The concern is that organizations wanting expedient answers and solutions to their workplace problems are often not willing to wait for the most appropriate research to be conducted. In contrast, I/O psychologists in academics who conduct much of the research are under pressure to publish and may often conduct laboratory-based studies which do not reflect actual work environments. These concerns are supported by the following evidence: while 77% of I/O psychologists surveyed spend at least some time in practice, only 65% conducted research (Howard, 1991). This lack of research is most noticeable among those I/O psychologists who practice independently and work for consulting firms: more than 60% of those surveyed who work as consultants indicated that they did no research.

While there is a tremendous amount of variety in the actual daily responsibilities and activities of I/O psychologists, the following descriptions provide samples of some of the work that is typically done by these people in different work settings.

James Murray:
Senior Consultant

James Murray specializes in incentive or reward systems and motivational programs, and has worked with many organizations to develop or modify the ways in which they motivate and reward their employees. For example, James recently worked with a large school system to develop a merit pay system. James first thoroughly studied the teachers' jobs and identified the characteristics and behaviors which distinguished the best teachers from those who were considered poor performers. He used this information to develop a set of guidelines and evaluation forms that supervisors can use to evaluate and provide feedback to the teachers on their performance. In addition, these forms can then be used to determine the merit raises that the particular teacher should get based on his or her performance. During this project, James worked with the school administrators and union leaders to develop a system that was satisfactory to both segments of the organization. In addition to the evaluation forms, James also worked with supervisors to teach them techniques that could be used to enhance motivation and morale among the teachers, and trained them to provide better support, reinforcement and feedback to teachers about their performance in the classroom.

Susan O'Neill:
Director of Selection and Recruiting

Susan O'Neill is an industrial/organizational psychologist working for a large chemical manufacturing firm. Susan's primary responsibilities are focused on developing and maintaining the company's recruiting and selection program. In this job, Susan first must be able to specify the responsibilities for a variety of jobs within the organization with detailed job descriptions. These descriptions clearly identify the tasks that employees will need to complete successfully in order to perform their jobs. After identifying the components of a given job, Susan chooses or develops the measures that will be useful in indentifying the best applicants. Sometimes she chooses standardized tests to measure aptitudes or abilities, other times she has developed an interview guide or simulation to be used when hiring people. When these measures are being chosen Susan must also demonstrate that they are valid: Do the tests and interviews help the company choose the people who will be good performers on the job? She may need to conduct a study with a large number of current employees or applicants to gather this information. An important part of Susan's job is to keep up-to-date on the numerous state and federal laws and regulations which affect the recruiting and hiring process including civil rights legislation and the Americans with Disabilities Act. She must also work with union representatives to make sure that the tests being used are fair to employees and allowed by the current contract. Finally, Susan is responsible for training the people administering these tests and interviews about how to adhere to these guidelines and regulations.

Sandra Baker:
Director of Training

Sandra Baker is an industrial/organizational psychologist working for a federal government agency. Within this organization, Sandra is the director and coordinator for the agency's training programs. In this position, Sandra oversees the development, implementation, and evaluation of the agency's training programs. To do her job successfully, Sandra must first understand the agency's goals for training and what it needs from its employees. Sandra and her associates need to study both the jobs being targeted for training and the individuals in those jobs. By comparing these components, Sandra and her colleagues can begin to understand what the employees can currently do and what they need to be able to do after training. Once the goals of the training program have been established, then Sandra and her co-workers develop the training materials for the program including the course content and the procedures or techniques that will be used to facilitate learning. This means writing training manuals, designing assignments, activities and simulations, and selecting or preparing readings or equipment. Sandra may actually conduct the training course or may give that responsibility to one of her associates. Once the training program is in place, Sandra and her associates must develop evaluation tools to determine if the training program is effective. First, they may create a test or simulation to determine if the trainees have mastered the material covered in the training program. Second, they may perform a larger evaluation in which those who are trained are compared to theose who have not been trained within the agency. If the program is effective, the trained individuals should perform better than those who have not been trained. Finally, after the evaluations are complete, Sandra is responsible for using that information to improve the training program.

Wallace Stevens:
Associate Professor of Psychology

Wallace Stevens is an industrial/organizational psychologist employed as an associate professor at a university. Wallace teaches courses in personnel psychology, workplace motivation, organizational behavior, and industrial/organizational psychology. In addition to his work in the classroom, Wallace conducts research on leadership styles. He is interested in the role that situational factors such as stressful working environments, employee level of expertise, and reward systems play in the effectiveness of different leaders. He has designed and conducted research to answer questions such as are directive leaders as effective as non-directive leaders for well-educated and professional employees? Does a stressful work environment always inhibit the effectiveness of a leader? In addition, Wallace occasionally consults for organizations that are near the university. He may prepare a two day leadership seminar for a local manufacturing firm or conduct a workshop for the city hospital on managing and motivating professional employees.

Section Summary:

Industrial and organizational psychologists study work behavior and apply psychological knowledge and principles to improve the work environment and enhance work effectiveness. The field of industrial and organizational psychology is founded in the scientist/practitioner model which emphasizes that the most effective practice in the workplace is founded on good research and that the best research is designed to answer questions found in the workplace. To understand this behavior and solve the workplace problems, I/O psychologists borrow from testing and psychometrics, motivation, personality and social psychology, learning theory and cognitive psychology. Industrial and organizational psychology is divided into two subfields: industrial psychology which focuses on using psychology to promote the most effective use of human resources within an organization, and organizational psychology emphasizes the importance of understanding organizations as groups of individuals and facilitating effective interactions between the members of those groups.

Industrial and organizational psychology developed soon after the turn of the century when psychologists were approached by employers to solve workplace problems such as how to choose employees who would be successful, how to train employees to do the work, and how to design jobs that were efficient and interesting. Somewhat later, I/O psychologists became interested in how attitudes such as job satisfaction affected work performance. Currently, I/O psychologists study many different aspects of the workplace including pre-employment testing, job training methods, workplace motivation, job design, job stress, retirement and organizational withdrawal, and organizational climate or culture. Industrial and organizational psychologists are typically employed in one of five primary work settings: private industry, academics, public organizations, consulting firms, and self-employed as consultants. In these jobs they function as researchers, practitioners, teachers, and managers. In the next section you will read about how industrial and organizational psychologists approach the first stage of the relationship between an employer and employee: recruitment and selection.

Recruitment and Selection: Hiring Qualified Employees.

What is the Purpose of Recruitment and Selection?

If you have ever looked for a job, gone through the application process and been hired, you have participated in what I/O psychologists call recruitment and selection. How did you find out about the job opening? Did you read the want ads? Did you hear from a friend who's brother or sister worked for the organization? Did you think the job sounded like fun? Did you have all the experience and skills required? Did you like what you read in the company's recruiting literature or their advertisements? What was the application process like? Did you have to collect reference letters from teachers and previous employers? Did you have to take a standardized test or actually perform some of the essential job activities? All of these activities are part of what I/O psychologists call recruitment and selection.

Recruitment and the selection process that follows may be considered the first stages of the relationship between the organization and the employee (Herriot, 1989). It is during this time that the potential applicant forms an impression about the organization, its policies, its employees and its products or services. Also during this time, the organization gathers initial information about the potential employee. The combined goal of these two processes is to find the best match between individual employees and their work. In principle, when the employee is well suited to the job and the job meets the employee's needs, both the employee and the employer benefit. The organization will have an effective person to perform the job and the individual will be in the job that he or she finds most interesting and that will use his or her potential fully.

Before initiating the recruitment process, an organization must evaluate its human resource needs. This effort may involve identifying the kinds of employees needed now and those are likely to be needed in the future by examining the labor market, specifying affirmative action goals, and examining the existing workforce. In the **recruitment** process, an organization attempts to maintain or expand its workforce by identifying and attracting a pool of qualified applicants for open positions. While organizations are recruiting, prospective employees are looking for jobs. Recruiting may focus on providing current employees with opportunities for advancement or job change or the emphasis may be on attracting new employees from outside the organization. Successful recruiting depends on three elements.

1. **The organization and applicant must share a common medium of communication.** For example, an applicant for a university teaching position in psychology must read the advertisements in the APA Monitor or hear about the position from a colleague.

2. **The applicant must perceive that he or she is qualified for the position.** Individuals must believe that they have the necessary skills, experience, and other qualifications to perform the job successfully.

3. **The applicant must be motivated to apply for the position.** Individuals must believe that the organization offers the opportunities that they seek. For example, one applicant may be finishing graduate school and is looking for a first job, while another may be dissatisfied with a current job and is seeking better employment.

Job Analysis: Describing Job Demands

Why Do a Job Analysis?

Once the applicants present themselves to the organization, the first step in the selection process is to define the qualifications needed to perform the job successfully. **Selection** means identifying the person to fill the job through hiring or promotion. Questions such as what are the essential features of good performance and what distinguishes an individual who is doing a good job from one who is doing a poor job must be answered before employees can be selected for a job. The job qualifications are typically defined through a technique called job analysis. **Job analysis** is a set of procedures designed to break a job into its essential tasks and most frequent activities; it identifies the resources people use to do their work and the results of good and bad performance (Guion, 1991).

Job analysis provides the foundation not only for selection, but is also an essential component in many activities conducted by an I/O psychologist. By having a thorough understanding of the job requirements, I/O psychologists can develop appropriate training programs, establish accurate performance evaluation systems, and recommend changes in the job which would make it more motivating or satisfying. A job analysis can also identify the procedures or technologies used by the job holder and describe the physical and social environment in which the work is performed (Harvey, 1991). Job analysis is also helpful in distinguishing between two or more different jobs. How is the job of the airplane pilot different from that of the flight engineer? Finally, a thorough job analysis can be used to understand how different experience, training, and ability may affect the level of performance on a particular job.

The procedures used in a job analysis also provide the foundation for a set of job specifications which identify the knowledge, skills, abilities, and other characteristics needed to perform those activities. These specifications can later be used to define acceptable standards of job performance, to suggest ways of evaluating job performance and ways to identify those individuals who are most likely to be good performers (Guion, 1991). Harvey (1991) identifies three characteristics of good job analysis procedures:

1. **Job analysis should focus on observable work behaviors or outcomes.** For example, a stockperson's job at a grocery store requires that the individual lift boxes weighing between 20 and 50 pounds, to bring those boxes to the appropriate section of the store, and to set up displays of those products.

2. **Job analysis should reflect the behaviors required for the job NOT necessarily those of the specific individuals who perform that job.** Individual job holders may behave in somewhat different manners such as performing tasks in different orders or using different methods. The job analysis should emphasize the goals and outcomes of activities more than the specific way in which those tasks are done.

3. **Job analysis should be verifiable and replicable.** The job analysis of sales positions in a department store should reveal similar results from salespeople in different stores.

Job Analysis Techniques

The information needed for a job analysis can be collected in a variety of ways. Research has not shown substantially different results when different methods are used to collect the data, but each of the methods has its strengths and weakness for different types of jobs (Hakel, 1986). Most job analysts use multiple methods to develop a comprehensive description of the job and to balance the strengths and weaknesses of the various methods. When beginning a job analysis, an I/O psychologist should first ask: Who will provide the information about the job? The primary requirement for selecting sources of information for the job analysis is to choose someone who has direct, current, and thorough experience with the job (Harvey, 1991). Just as most job analysts use multiple methods to collect data about the job, they frequently rely on a variety of sources for that data.

The psychologist may approach **job incumbents**: the individuals who currently hold the job being analyzed. These individuals actually perform the job and are most likely to be familiar with the behaviors that they engage in every day. Unfortunately there are some drawbacks to using job incumbents. First, the incumbents must have enough experience to have mastered the job being analyzed and therefore to describe what it entails. Inexperienced employees providing job analysis data may still be learning the job requirements, may omit important details about the job or may emphasize work activities that become less important with practice. Second, the individuals providing job analysis data need to have the verbal ability to clearly describe their activities and performance goals to the job analyst; this can be a problem at lower levels of an organization. Third, the employees need to be motivated to participate in the process. Job incumbents may feel that they are wasting their time completing questionnaires or being interviewed when they could be getting their work done. Finally, job incumbents may be sensitive to the purposes behind the job analysis and modify their responses accordingly. For example, if a job analysis will be used to determine the compensation for that job, the incumbents are likely to over-emphasize the difficulty of the job or the time needed to complete an assignment. Under these circumstances every job is portrayed as extremely important to the organization's performance. In contrast, if the analysis will be used to establish performance standards and production quotas, the employees may be tempted to perform the job more slowly so that later comparisons will be favorable.

Supervisors can be a second source of information for the job analysis. Like incumbents, supervisors are likely to be very familiar with the jobs they oversee and understand the essential functions of those jobs. In addition, supervisors are likely to have higher levels of verbal ability, and can more clearly articulate their observations about the work that is being done. Unfortunately, supervisors may also place a low priority on the job analysis and therefore be less willing to put time and effort into questionnaires or interviews. Supervisors may also share some of the biases found in the incumbents about the significance or difficulty of the job being analyzed.

Trained job analysts may be used as a third source for job analysis data. The advantages to this source are obvious: these individuals have the expertise to articulate the job activities clearly and systematically in the language and form needed by the I/O psychologist. The drawbacks to using trained job analysts are equally obvious: they are less familiar with the job itself and may need a substantial amount of time to develop a thorough understanding of the work being done. Also, because they tend to know less about the actual job requirements, professional job analysts are more likely to rely on job stereotypes when gathering the data about a job, they may be more likely attend to information which confirms their expectations, and to ignore information which is contradictory (Harvey, 1991).

Finally, clients (individuals within or outside the organization who receive products or services from the job incumbents) may be used as a source for job analysis data. While these individuals may not be able to clearly articulate the ways in which the job is performed, they should be able to specify the outcomes that are necessary or desirable. For example, customers in a restaurant could describe what distinguishes a good waiter from a poor one, or a salesperson could describe the type of information and materials that would be most useful to receive from the marketing team.

Combining information from two or more of these sources allows the job analyst to gather different perspectives about the essential features of the job; the analyst may compare what the employee believes are the most important and most frequent responsibilities with what the supervisor feels is essential for good performance, and with clients' expectations. In addition, by gathering data from a large number of sources, the I/O psychologist is more likely to identify the facets of the job that are most affected by different levels of experience and those behaviors that distinguish good performers from poor performers on the job.

Once an I/O psychologist has chosen the sources of the job analysis data, he or she must select the methods for gathering these data. The most common job analysis procedures involve questionnaires and interviews. Initial interviews will typically be unstructured and focus the job's primary responsibilities. From these initial unstructured interviews the I/O psychologist may develop a questionnaire, a more detailed structured interview, or choose a standardized job analysis measure that can be applied to any one of a variety of positions. These interviews or questionnaires are then administered to a larger group of employees, supervisors and/or clients.

There are many standardized instruments available for this purpose including the Position Analysis Questionnaire (PAQ), and the Job Element Inventory (JEI) that can be used to analyze any job (McCormick, Jeanneret & Mecham, 1972 ; Harvey, Friedman, Hakel & Cornelius, 1988). For example, the PAQ is a structured job analysis questionnaire that analyzes jobs using 187 generic work behaviors. These behaviors are divided into six categories:

1. Information input: Where and how does the job incumbent get the information needed to perform the job? A doctor, for example, may gather information from a patient's medical records and charts, small medical instruments such as a thermometer or stethoscope, and large medical equipment such as heart monitors.

2. Mental processes: Does the job require reasoning, decision making, planning, and information-processing? An engineer might interpret computer printouts or record environmental conditions throughout the day.

3. Work output: What physical activities are required on the job, and what tools or equipment are used? A landscaper might use shovels, wheelbarrows and grading equipment and is required to lift objects weighing 50 to 100 pounds.

4. Relationships with other persons: How and with whom does the incumbent interact while on the job? A police officer might have to advise citizens on safety precautions, interview suspects, and settle disputes between neighbors.

5. Job context: What is the job's physical and social environment? A television journalist may be required to work outdoors and be subject to changing weather conditions, or to enter dangerous areas when reporting on violence or natural disasters.

6. Other job characteristics: What other job features are relevant? A counselor will need to be licensed by the state and a computer analyst may be on call one night per week and one weekend per month (Mecham, McCormick & Jeanneret,1977).

The primary advantage to methods such as the PAQ is that they are standardized so that jobs can be compared across organizations and occupations. One disadvantage however, of this method is that because the questionnaire is generic, the questions may be interpreted in different ways by the individuals completing it. While this problem may be solved by creating a unique questionnaire based on interviews and other prior information, a large amount of time and effort may be involved in doing this for each job that must be analyzed.

In addition to questionnaires and interviews, a job analyst may also observe individuals actually performing their jobs. This method is advantageous when employees may have difficulty describing how they do something because the tasks have become too automatic (think about how you would describe in detail, something that you do frequently such as take a shower or make your breakfast). In addition, you may remember from your study of memory processes that implicit memory (memory for skills) is hard to translate into a set of facts that describe the performance of that skill. Third, job incumbents may describe how the job should be completed and not necessarily how they actually do their work; using observation, the job analyst can record the activities of the individual incumbents and their frequency. One shortcoming of the observation method is that it may be less useful for jobs which require a lot of thinking, reasoning, or problem solving but involve little observable activity, or for those that are dangerous and may be difficult to observe and describe accurately such as a police officer or firefighter.

Finally, in some cases the job analyst may actually perform the job in order to gather the necessary information. This method is feasible only if the job does not require substantial skills or training. For example, this method would not be realistic for many highly skilled jobs such as a nurse, engineer, laboratory technician or pilot.

Outcomes and Results From a Job Analysis

Once the job analysis has been completed, the analyst develops a detailed job description and identifies a set of job specifications. One common framework for the job description includes listing a set of major responsibilities or duties: activities which occupy at least five percent of the time on the job. For example, a manager of a grocery store is responsible for setting the schedule for the store's employees. The next level of detail in the job description involves generating a list of tasks that combine to form those major responsibilities. Preparing the week's schedule involves determining how many cashiers, stockpeople, bakery, deli and meat department employees are needed in the store throughout the week. Finally, this list of tasks can be broken down into a set of job specifications: the knowledge, skills, abilities and other characteristics that are required to complete those tasks. The manager must understand the area's shopping patterns, have planning skills, and knowledge of the restrictions on length of workday that are included in the employees' contract. Table 1 shows the results from a job analysis of a secretary's job outlining the major responsibilities and the essential job specifications (knowledge, skills, abilities, and other characteristics) that would be needed to successfully perform the job.

Identifying Job Performance Criteria: Defining Good Performance

Once the job analysis has been completed and the job description written, the next step in the selection process is to define good performance on that job and to select ways to measure that performance. An organization expects that the applicants who are hired will do the job better than those who were not hired. **Job performance criteria** describe what it means to do the job well and imply accurate ways to measure job performance. The performance criteria chosen by an organization should reflect its goals and values. They specifically define the desired outcomes

26

Table 1
Results From a Job Analysis of a Secretary:

Major Responsibilities
1. Word processing of letters, reports, papers
2. Answering phone calls
3. Keeping and filing records
4. Scheduling appointments
5. Ordering supplies
6. Compiling information from a variety of sources for reports or decision making.

Job specifications

Extremely important:

reading skills
ability to follow written instructions
ability to follow oral instructions
detail orientation for inspecting written work
anticipating time needed to complete tasks
anticipating amount of supplies needed
typing and word-processing skills
ability to work with distractions
ability to apply job and organizational knowledge
oral communication skills: routine information
interpersonal skills for interactions with a variety of individuals

listening skills
planning skills
organization skills
short term memory skills
hand-ear coordination
fine motor coordination

Important:

transcribing skills
coordinating the activities of others
ability to work under deadlines
reasoning skills

analyzing information
negotiating skills
problem solving skills
intermediate math skills

Education and training required:
High School Education

1 to 3 years of experience

for a job. Job performance criteria reflect what the organization needs for the individuals in this job to do well. Good performance criteria reflect the individual's performance and not factors which are out of his or her control such as resource availability or another employee's work.

Obviously, job performance criteria are used by employers for more than the selection process. Once these criteria have been established, specific measures of them can be developed, creating a performance appraisal system. **Performance appraisal systems** are specific ways in which employees' job performance can be measured and evaluated. These evaluations are used to make personnel decisions such as promotions or terminations. Performance appraisal provides feedback to the employees about the strengths and weaknesses of performance, recognizing good work and suggesting areas which need improvement. These evaluations are frequently used to determine levels of compensation such as merit raises or year-end bonuses. Finally, performance appraisal can identify training needs. Do employees lack specific skills which would enhance their performance?

Choosing Selection Measures: What is a "Good" Predictor?

Having identified the job specifications and outlined the job performance criteria, the I/O psychologist is ready to choose **predictors**. Predictors are measures used in the selection process that should correctly identify those applicants who will be good performers; the results from these measures predict future success on the job. When choosing a selection measure, an organization must first know that it is a "good" measurement tool. Most importantly, measures used in selection should have reliability and validity.

Reliability

If a measure is reliable, the results from that measure are consistent. For example, if an applicant is interviewed twice under similar conditions, the ratings from those two interviews should be comparable. Reliability can be estimated in a variety of ways. **Test-retest reliability** is determined by giving a group of individuals a test once, and then giving that same group of people the same test later. Scores on these two tests should be similar and the correlation between the two sets of scores should be strong and positive.

A second technique for estimating a measure's reliability is **alternate forms reliability**. To establish alternate forms reliability, the I/O psychologist must have two versions of the same test. These two tests should cover the same content, use the same format, and have equal difficulty levels. To establish alternate forms reliability, the one version of the test is given to a group of people, and at some point later in time, the second version is given to those same individuals. Like test-retest reliability, individuals' scores on the two versions of the test should be similar and the correlation between the two sets of scores should be strong and positive.

A third reliability estimate that is frequently applied to selection measures is **inter-rater reliability**. This type of reliability indicates that individuals will get similar scores when evaluated by two or more different judges. Inter-rater reliability is particularly important for interviews, work samples, and other situational tests in which the applicant's performance is rated or judged by one or more evaluators. An organization using subjective ratings made by judges needs to know that the different raters will make similar judgments about individuals.

Validity

A second characteristic that is essential for a selection tool is **validity**. A valid test measures what it is supposed to measure. To be considered useful and valid, scores on the selection measure should be related to scores on the job performance criterion. There are various ways to validate a test. In one validation method, called criterion-related validity, the I/O psychologist must collect data from a sample of applicants for whom both the test scores and the performance ratings are known. Criterion-related validity can be estimated in two different ways: concurrent criterion related validity and predictive criterion related validity.

When a measure has **predictive criterion-related validity**, scores on the test predict job performance after the applicants are hired. For example, if an organization wants to use a personality test such as the Guilford-Zimmerman Temperament Survey (GZTS) to select managers, the I/O psychologist would want to know if people who score high on the sociability and energy and ascendance scales are the people who would be the best managers once they were hired (Guilford, Zimmerman, & Guilford, 1976). To establish this kind of validity the psychologist could give the personality test to a group of applicants. Some of these applicants would be hired for the management jobs (the personality test should not be used in this decision) and one year later collect some measure of their job performance (the actual time between administering the measure and measuring the job performance criterion will vary). If the personality test is valid for predicting job performance of managers, then the individuals who got the highest test scores on those scales should be those individuals who are performing the best after they were hired.

A second alternative is to establish **concurrent criterion-related validity**. For this type of validity, the psychologist would give the personality test to a group of managers currently working for the organization and collect information about their current job performance. If the test is valid, those who have the highest scores on the sociability and energy and ascendance scales of the GZTS should also be the better performers.

Obviously, there are some problems associated with each of these methods. For the predictive criterion related validity it may be difficult to convince the organization to hire individuals without using this predictor, this is especially true if the organization does not have an effective selection system in place. The organization will incur the costs of recruiting and hiring, and the potential costs of mistakes made by the individuals who were hired but who cannot successfully do the job. This problem is avoided by establishing concurrent validity, but the test is used differently than it would be in the selection process since the test is given to people who have already been hired. These employees may have changed in important ways since the time they were applicants. The organization should assume that employees develop more skills or improve their performance after being hired and will therefore get different scores on the measure than they would have as applicants. Second, by only using current employees the I/O psychologist has left out important groups of individuals: those who are not successful enough to stay on the job or to be hired in the first place, and those who quit for various reasons. This problem is known as **restriction of range**. The sample on which the test is validated includes many more individuals with high scores on the performance criterion than would be expected in the applicant sample. Using a more homogeneous sample to validate the test will typically lower the observed correlation between the test scores and the job performance criterion. Recently, some researchers argue that in practice restriction of range does not significantly alter validity estimates but these issues are still being debated (Schmidt, Ones, & Hunter, 1992). Finally, many predictors have a significant weakness when they are compared to the job performance criterion. Interviews, achievement tests, and

31

work samples typically measure the applicants' highest possible level of performance. In contrast, most performance criteria focus on a summary or average of the applicants' performance. So while predictors are measures of maximum performance - the best that an applicant can do, most performance criteria are measures of typical performance - what an applicant usually does.

Classic Validity Theory

When choosing the predictors to be used in a selection system, an organization should determine if the tools used will improve the decisions made about applicants and if the money spent developing and using these tools will be saved by hiring fewer unqualified people. The value of including a measure as part of a selection process depends on its reliability and validity. Other factors also affect the usefulness of particular measures for making decisions about applicants. I/O psychologists have used a variety of statistical and theoretical models to understand the different decisions and consequences that are possible in the selection process. In the classical validity approach, the I/O psychologist would first establish the predictive criterion-related validity of the test or the combination of tools used during the selection process using the methods described earlier. For example, if an organization wants to use a structured interview in its hiring program for managers it would first establish the predictive criterion related validity of that interview. The relationship between the applicants' scores on the interview and their later performance scores can be shown in a scatterplot. Figure 2 provides an example of this relationship. Each point in the scatterplot represents two scores for each individual: the interview score is plotted on the x axis, and the subsequent performance score is plotted on the y axis. The psychologist combines this information with knowledge of the organization's minimum performance standard for its managers. This minimum performance is called **the criterion cutoff**. In this example, the criterion cutoff is a performance rating of 2; managers with a

32

performance rating above 2 are retained by the company while those with a score 2 or below are asked to leave. The organization can also establish a cutoff score on the interview measure: for this example it is a score of 12 and is called the **predictor cutoff**. Applicants with an interview score above 12 will be hired while those with a score of 12 or below will not.

These two cutoff scores create four separate quadrants in the graph which represent four different types of decisions and consequences for the individuals in this sample. First, there is a group of people who scored above 2 on the structured interview, and who also get a performance rating above 2. These individuals are classified as **correct acceptances**; they have been hired because they score high enough on the predictor and they will be successful employees. Second, there is a group of individuals who have a performance rating above a two, but who did not score above 12 on the interview. These individuals are classified as **incorrect rejections** because the organization would not normally hire them based on their test score but they are successful managers. Third, there is a group of individuals who score below 12 on the interview and also get a performance rating below two. These individuals are labeled **correct rejections** because they would not be hired on the basis of their test scores and they are not successful managers. Finally, there is a group of people who score above 12 on the interview, but do not receive a performance rating above a 2. These individuals are considered **incorrect acceptances** because they would be hired on the basis of their test scores but they are not successful as managers.

The proportion of individuals in these four categories depends on a number of variables. The first of these variables is the base rate. The **base rate** is the proportion of people who can successfully perform the job. If the base rate is high (90% of all applicants can successfully perform the job), then the organization will have few incorrect acceptances. In contrast, if the base rate is low

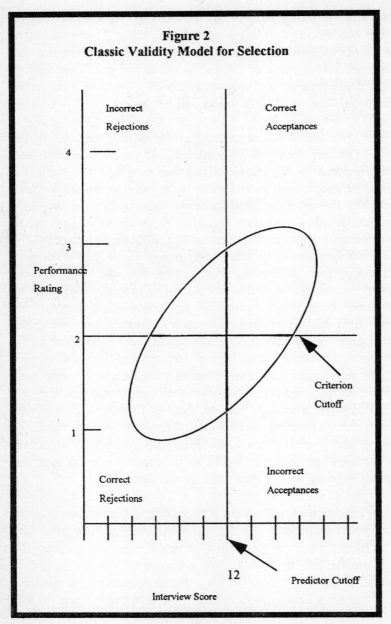

Figure 2
Classic Validity Model for Selection

Incorrect Rejections

Correct Acceptances

Performance Rating

Criterion Cutoff

Correct Rejections

Incorrect Acceptances

12

Predictor Cutoff

Interview Score

(15% of all applicants can successfully perform the job) then the organization will have few incorrect rejections. The second of these factors is the **selection ratio**, the proportion of applicants who will be hired. The selection ratio equals the number of individuals hired divided by the total number of applicants. If this ratio is low (1 out 100 for example) then the organization can move the predictor cutoff to the right and minimize the number of incorrect acceptances. The tradeoff for this choice is that there are more incorrect rejections (people who could have been successful but did not pass the selection test). When there is a large number of applicants for a small number of job openings, the organization can take only the very best applicants.

In contrast, if the selection ratio is high (1/5), then the organization may be forced to move the predictor cutoff to the left and reduce the number of incorrect rejections. The tradeoff in this situation is that there will be more incorrect acceptances (people who are hired but who will not be effective managers). When there are many jobs available but few applicants, the organization may need to hire some of the applicants with lower predictor scores in order to have as many successful employees as they will need. Obviously, the organization wants to maximize the proportion of correct acceptances and correct rejections and minimize the proportion of incorrect rejections and incorrect acceptances. Both of these decisions are potentially costly to the organization. Incorrect rejections represent lost productivity because the people would have been successful employees. In addition, these individuals may go to work for a competitor. Similarly, incorrect acceptances cost the organization money in the form of training that does not pay off, salary that is paid to an unsuccessful worker, and other expenses that are used on an employee who is not helping to meet organizational objectives. The best way to simultaneously reduce both types of bad decisions is to use a measure that has a higher validity. This reduces the proportion of people who are in those two categories because the test gives a more accurate prediction of the applicants' job performance.

Using More Than One Predictor

Most organizations will use more than a single predictor in their selection process. It is typical for employers to combine the information obtained about an applicant from multiple predictors such as an interview, an application, and a cognitive ability test. When multiple predictors are used, the organization must have a way of combining that information about each applicant systematically. I/O psychologists have identified three methods of combining the information from multiple predictors to make selection decisions. The first option is **multiple regression**. In multiple regression the scores from each of the measures is assigned a weight based on its relationship with the job performance criterion and the other predictors. A total score is developed from that weighted combination of predictor scores that reflects the applicants' performance on all the selection measures. The applicants are selected on the basis of this composite score. The primary disadvantage to this method is that a high score on one of the predictors may compensate for a low score on the others when those skills do not compensate for each other on the job.

A second method for combining information from more than one predictor is to use **multiple cutoffs**. When this technique is used, applicants must attain a minimum score on each of the predictors in order to be considered for the position. A slight variation of this practice is called **multiple hurdles** in which the applicant completes one predictor at a time and a cutoff is set for each predictor. If the applicant does not meet the cutoff score on a predictor he or she is dropped from the applicant pool and does not take any additional tests.

For example, if you are applying for a sales position with an insurance company, you might first send a resume and cover letter. From the applicant pool, the company chooses 15 individuals whose resume's reflect the qualifications for the job. If you are in that group of 15 applicants, you are asked to take a personality test and a cognitive ability test. If you score above the minimum required for the job, then you are asked to come in for a structured interview. If more applicant remain in the pool than are needed by the organization, multiple regression may be used to identify the applicants with the highest predicted performance. The primary difficulty with using the multiple hurdles and multiple cutoffs approaches is that it may be difficult to establish a valid cutoff score for the various predictors. The organization must justify hiring an individual who scores a 26 while rejecting an individual who scores a 25.

Utility Analysis
A variety of researchers have attempted to describe the validity of a selection system in terms of the amount saved by the organization because it is able to make more accurate hiring decisions. In general, regardless of the method for computing these estimates the results suggest that a valid selection program is cost effective for the organization. **Utility analysis** involves estimating the costs associated with a new selection technique and comparing that to the expected savings from the introduction of that technique. The degree to which a hiring process is cost effective will depend on a variety of factors including the dollar value of the job for which applicants are being hired, how long they are likely to stay with the organization, the selection ratio, the cost of the selection program, and its validity. The savings will be greater to the extent that a job that has a high dollar value, the selection ratio is high, the incumbents will remain with the organization for a long period of time, the cost of the selection program is low, and its validity of the measures used is high.

Particular Selection Measures

Generally, an I/O psychologist will select or create a collection of predictors that can be used during the hiring process. The combination of measures used such as interviews, aptitude tests, or work sample tests should predict applicants' later job performance. Those who are successful during the interview, get high scores on the aptitude test, or successfully complete the work sample should later get good ratings by their supervisors or have higher levels of objective performance than those who did not. The combination of measures will differ across jobs and organizations depending on the demands of the jobs. For example Ash, Slora and Britton (1990) surveyed state and urban police departments to identify the various selection methods used. Ninety-two percent used tests of cognitive ability, 68% used personality tests, 35% used biographical data questionnaires and 80% used measures of physical strength and agility. In contrast, organizations selecting managers might use personality tests, interviews, and work sample tests. The following section describes some of the most popular selection measures and the strengths and weaknesses of each.

Interviews
Interviews are one of the most popular selection tools. They can be classified as either unstructured or structured. In an unstructured interview, the interviewer is free to ask the questions that he or she feels are appropriate for a particular applicant; applicants for the same position will not necessarily be asked the same questions. The primary weakness to this approach is that applicants cannot be easily compared because they did not all respond to the same kinds of questions. In addition, an interviewer is more likely to miss important information about an applicant or to emphasize information that may not be essential for choosing the most qualified person because the questions asked may not reflect the most crucial job demands. Some

researchers have found relatively high predictive validities for unstructured interviews (.40) (Schmidt, Ones and Hunter, 1992) while most others suggest that this interview format is problematic and has very low validity (Ulrich and Trumbo, 1965; Schmitt, 1976; Motowidlo, Carter, Dunnette, Tippens, Werner, Burnett and Vaughan, 1992).

Most I/O psychologists argue that structured interview formats are more useful than more conversational or unstructured interviews (Guion, 1991). Structured interviews are designed so that all applicants for a given position are observed systematically. When using a structured interview, an interview guide is prepared for the interviewers which describes the nature of the questions to be asked, the elements of the applicants' answers that should be evaluated, and the standards for judging those responses. The interviewer does not have to decide what questions to ask and how to evaluate the applicant, but he or she decides when follow-up questions should be asked and when there is enough information to make the necessary judgements. This technique allows for meaningful comparisons across applicants because they respond to similar questions about the same job responsibilities.

A specific example of a structured interview is the structured behavioral interview developed by Motowidlo et al., (1992) for management and marketing positions in the telecommunications industry. This interview format has five specific characteristics.

1. The interview content is founded on categories of behavior that can be identified in a job analysis.

2. The questions focus on how interviewees have handled past situations that are similar to those that might occur on the job.

3. The interview may ask follow-up questions about the details of the situation, the applicant's behavior, or the outcome of the event.

4. The interviewer takes notes during the interview and reviews those notes before rating the responses on a set of standardized, behavioral scales.

5. The ratings are combined to yield an overall rating of interview performance.

In a study of approximately 500 participants, this interview format showed excellent inter-rater reliability and both predictive and criterion-related validity. To establish concurrent validity, 164 managers from seven companies were interviewed. The participants were asked to pretend that they were applicants for their current jobs and to answer the questions from that point of view. The interview ratings were significantly correlated with job performance ratings on five criteria: interpersonal skills, problem solving abilities, leadership, communication skills, and overall performance.

To establish the predictive validity of this interview, 195 applicants were interviewed over a two year period. Again interview scores were correlated with performance ratings that were given after these applicants had been hired. The correlations were again significant between scores on the interview and subsequent performance ratings. In addition, these researchers demonstrated that this particular interview format does not have significant overlap with measures of cognitive ability or other characteristics that might be measured more readily by a standardized test. Also, the study showed only small differences in the interview scores on the basis of race or sex which indicates that this interview is not biased against particular groups of employees.

One subset of structured interviews are designated **situational interviews**. In a situational interview, the applicants are asked questions about events that are essential for success or failure on the job known as critical incidents. Applicants are presented with a situation and asked to describe how they would behave under those circumstances. For example, an applicant for a customer service representative with a long distance telephone service might be asked how he would handle an angry customer who wants a refund and who is ready to terminate his relationship with this company. Although there has been some concern that individuals will respond as they think they should, rather than how they would actually respond, Latham and Saari (1984) found that there is a high degree of correspondence between what individuals say they would do and what supervisors report that they actually do in those situations.

Although the content of structured interviews will vary from one organization to the next, the format typically will have some common features (Hakel, 1982). What are you likely to experience as an applicant being given a structured interview? The interview is likely to begin with an introduction during which you exchange names with the interviewer and have a casual conversation. The goal of this step is to make you more comfortable before the job-related questions begin. Next, the interviewer should tell you about the interview sequence. During most of the interview you will probably answer questions about your education, previous work experience, and your skills that are relevant to the job. After asking these questions, the interviewer is likely to describe the job that you have applied for and will allow time for you to ask questions about the job or organization. The interviewer should close the interview with an outline of the next steps in the decision process and the date by which a decision is likely to be made. Finally, after the interview, the interviewer

41

should complete his or her notes and write a summary of your performance during the interview.

As you can see from this outline, interviews should also provide an opportunity for the applicant to gather information about the organization. The interviewer is responsible for making the organization look attractive to the applicant and for providing a thorough description of the job. Applicants may frequently have inflated and unrealistic expectations about the positions for which they are applying. Recruiters and company literature may present a very positive view of the organization and the particular job being applied for, and overlook many of the problems or difficulties that an employee can encounter after taking the job. Some researchers have suggested that both applicants and organizations are best served if the applicant receives balanced and realistic information about the job during the selection process (Wanous, 1977).

Realistic job previews (RJP) are an attempt to provide applicants with more precise information about the jobs they are applying for so that they may better estimate the degree to which the job will meet their personal needs and goals. RJPs are designed to provide an accurate description of a job's demands and responsibilities, the type of work to be done, and the likelihood of career advancement. If an RJP were included as part of your selection process, you might discuss stressful work periods such as deadlines for a journalist or a salesperson, experience potentially unpleasant working conditions such as noise or weather for an airport employee, or see a videotape which depicts some of the drawbacks to the job you are applying for. RJPs should present information that will lower overly positive expectations and raise overly negative expectations (Meglino, DeNisi, Youngblood, & Williams, 1988). Wanous (1977) found that when the expectations of job applicants were lowered to a more realistic level, job acceptance rates were lower,

42

but job satisfaction was higher and turnover was lower among those who took the jobs. Providing realistic information about a job seems to be beneficial for both applicants and employers in the long run because the applicants who take the job are more satisfied and more likely to stay. This effect is more obvious for complex jobs than simple or routine jobs (Rynes, 1991). Researchers are currently trying to understand when and why RJPs reduce the likelihood that employees will quit their jobs and enhance overall job satisfaction. Both of these effects will make the selection process more useful to both the applicants and the employer.

While interviews are one of the most popular selection techniques there are a number of concerns about them. First, negative information about the applicant seems to weigh more heavily than positive information in the interview (Schmitt, 1976). Second, the reliability and validity of interviews can be low if the interviewers are not adequately trained. While a given interviewer is likely to be consistent, the differences between interviewers can be substantial. To reduce this effect, interviewer training should focus on understanding the job requirements, agreeing on how to combine information gathered during the interview, and agreeing on what represents a good answer, a fair answer, and a poor answer from an applicant. Finally, most research suggests that interviews should be used to collect information that is not easily obtained from other sources. In other words, it is not necessary to use an interview to find out about an applicant's education or work experience since this information could be easily obtained on an application. Similarly, trying to estimate cognitive abilities or specific aptitudes during an interview would probably not be useful since these skills and characteristics can be measured with paper and pencil tests. Interviews are probably best suited to gathering information about interpersonal skills and work motivation (Ulrich & Trumbo, 1965).

Cognitive ability measures

A second set of selection tools is cognitive ability tests. Some of these tests measure various aspects of general intelligence and may require the applicant to respond to items that require memory, problems solving skills, and analysis. Cognitive ability tests used in selection include the Wonderlic Personnel Inventory, the Miller Analogies Test, the Test of Non-Verbal Reasoning, the General Aptitude Test Battery (GATB) and the Armed Services Vocational Aptitude Battery (ASVAB). Some researchers have argued that general ability measures should be used because they are good predictors of job performance across a variety of jobs and organizations (Schmidt et al, 1992). In a recent large study of army jobs, Project A, ability measures predicted ratings of several overall performance criteria (McHenry, Hough, Toquam, Hanson, & Ashworth, 1990). Similarly, in a series of studies evaluating the relationships between leader intelligence and group performance (Fiedler, 1989; Gibson, Fiedler & Daniels, 1990; Murphy, Blythe & Fiedler, 1990) researchers found that the nature of this relationship depends on the leader's management style. Directive leaders get the best performance from their groups when they have high cognitive ability and less directive leaders get the best performance from their groups when they have lower cognitive ability. Other organizations use specific ability tests such as verbal ability tests, spatial ability tests or mechanical abilities tests to measure job-related abilities.

Personality Tests

Personality tests are also frequently used in the selection process. Historically, personality theory and measurement developed from a clinical perspective and focused on those aspects of personality which could distinguish patients with psychological disorders from normal individuals. Many of the tests developed for this purpose are not generally useful in personnel selection. In contrast, tests designed to measure interpersonal differences that affect typical social interactions such as the Personal

Characteristics Inventory (PCI), the Guilford-Zimmerman Temperament Survey (GZTS), the 16 PF, the California Psychological Inventory (CPI), and the Hogan Personality Inventory (HPI) have become more popular in recent years (Hogan, 1991). Many of these tests support the five factor model of personality (Digman, 1990; Goldberg, 1990) and have been used to predict job performance in a variety of occupational categories including military jobs, management and sales (Hogan, 1991; Barrick & Mount, 1993) The five factor model describes personality in terms of five basic components or factors:

1. **extroversion**: sociable, talkative, assertive
2. **agreeableness**: good natured, cooperative, trusting
3. **conscientiousness:** responsible, dependable, persistent, achievement-oriented
4. **neuroticism or emotional stability:** relaxed, secure
5. **openness to experience:** imaginative, creative intellectual.

The conscientiousness factor seems to be a good predictor across a a variety of jobs (Barrick & Mount, 1993). The extroversion scale is a good predictor of performance in jobs such as sales and management. The other factors do not function as well as predictors of job performance. In a study of 150 managers Barrick & Mount (1993) found that the relationship between these personality variables and job performance is moderated by the amount of autonomy that the individual has. They found that managers who score high on the conscientiousness and extroversion factors will perform best in jobs where they have a lot of independence and can determine how to do their work. In contrast, those who score high on the agreeableness factor perform better in jobs where they have less independence and little discretion in how the work can be done. In Project A, the conscientiousness factor predicted employee effort, ratings of leaderships and personal discipline (Hough, Eaton, Dunnette, Kamp, & McCloy, 1990).

While the use of personality measures in selection has increased over the last few years, not all I/O psychologists agree about the usefulness of personality tests for selection. One of the major concerns that has been raised about using these tests is that they may represent an invasion of the applicant's privacy. Another problem with personality tests is the susceptibility to faking. Individuals taking these tests can create a more favorable score when instructed to do so (Hogan, 1991).

Honesty Tests and Drug Screening

In addition to global measures of personality, honesty or integrity tests have also been used in the selection process. These tests have become particularly popular since the Employee Polygraph Protection Act was passed in 1988. This law prohibits most private sector employees from using polygraph tests in their hiring procedures. Polygraph or lie detector tests are designed to indicate when people are lying or telling the truth by measuring physiological reactions to a series of questions. Paper and pencil honesty or integrity tests typically measure attitudes about theft and dishonesty and self reports of actual theft or illegal activity. Some integrity tests however, resemble personality measures and should predict theft, drug use or absenteeism on the basis of a broad range of attitudes and behaviors which might be associated with drug use, illegal activity, or other harmful behaviors. To date, most of these tests do not seem to be accurate measures or good predictors of future job performance.

Pre-employment drug screening is also included in the hiring procedures of many organizations. These tests are typically in the form of urinalysis but some organizations will use self-report data (Normand, Salyards & Mahoney, 1990; Cascio, 1991). There has been a tremendous amount of debate about the usefulness and fairness of drug screening during selection and as a condition of continued employment. Normand et al., (1990) conducted a

46

thorough investigation of drug screening as a predictor of subsequent job performance. In this study the researchers set out to establish the validity and utility of drug screening as a selection tool. More specifically, they investigated the relationship between pre-employment drug screening results and the employees' absenteeism, turnover, injury, and accident rates after they had been hired. To evaluate these tests the researchers collected data from over 5000 job applicants for the U.S. Postal Service at 21 sites across the U.S. Physicians at each of these sites collected urine samples from the applicants after informing them that part of the sample would be used for a drug test. Applicants knew that the individual test results would not be considered in the hiring decisions. The physicians also collected self-report data about the prior and current use of prescription and over-the-counter medications so that these samples could be checked. The samples were initially analyzed for eight different drug types using EMIT, an enzyme multiplied immunoassay technique and positive samples were analyzed with a second, more precise procedure, gas chromotography/mass spectrometry. In addition, later the researchers collected four types of job performance data on those applicants who were hired: absenteeism, turnover, injuries, and accidents. Absenteeism was measured as a ratio of total hours absent for sick leave, leave without pay and absence without official leave to the total scheduled work hours. Turnover was separated into voluntary turnover (those individuals who resigned or were transferred) and involuntary (those employees who were fired). Injuries and accidents were identified through forms required after a work-related injury or accident has occurred.

A quality control study showed no false positives (testing positive for drug use when they have *not* been used) after the two screening methods were used and only four false negatives (*not* identifying drug use when they *have* been used). These results are considered satisfactory because of the negative consequences for an individual of false positives but not for false negatives. These researchers found that employees who had positive drug screen results missed significantly more of their total work time after they were hired than those who had negative drug screen results. Those with positive results were absent on average 6.63% of their total work hours while those with negative results missed 4.16% of their total work time on average. In addition, applicants who had positive drug screen results were 5.5 times more likely to have been fired than those with negative results. There were no significant relationships between drug screen results and either injury or accident rates.

Using these results, the researchers conducted a utility analysis to identify the cost and benefits to using drug screening during the selection process. Considering the cost of the drug testing program, the costs associated with turnover (training, recruiting, hiring a replacement), and the cost of lost work time due to absenteeism, the researchers estimated that the Postal Service could save more than 52 million dollars over a ten year period for a single group of applicants. These results suggest that pre-employment drug screens can be a useful component of a selection program when conducted properly. The results of the drug screens predicted at least two outcomes that are costly to the organization in this study: involuntary turnover and absenteeism. These results suggest that using drug screens can help to minimize the likelihood that applicants who are hired will become problem employees. However, while these tests can be good predictors of future performance and on-the-job behavior, they should not be over-emphasized in the selection process (Cascio, 1991). Like all other selection tools these tests should be considered in light of all other information gathered about the applicant.

Work Samples

A fifth category of selection measures is work sample tests. In a work sample test the applicant is asked to perform some of the tasks that will be required on the job. These tests typically require applicants to demonstrate proficiency on important job tasks under standardized and realistic conditions. Work sample tests are most appropriate for experienced workers who already have the skills needed to perform the job. The tasks chosen for this test are selected from the job analysis and are frequently those tasks that are considered most important for success on the job. For example, an applicant for a teacher's position might be asked to prepare and present a lesson for a class, an engineer may be asked to identify the source of a major equipment malfunction in a manufacturing procedure, or an executive may be asked to prepare a business report. One of the primary concerns about using work sample tests is that they measure what the employee can do and not necessarily what he or she will do. The applicant might put more effort toward the work sample than to the tasks when they are assigned on the job. The teacher might prepare more thoroughly or design more activities for the students, the engineer might be more systematic about identifying the sources of error, and the executive may put more effort into the business report.

Situational tests are a slight variation of work sample tests. These exercises simulate actual job tasks and environments. A popular situational test is the **in-basket test** used in the selection of managers. In a typical in-basket test, the applicant responds to a variety of items that would be in an in-basket for the position. The in-basket might contain reports, memos, and phone messages that might be expected on the job. The applicant might need to write a letter or memo, or organize and plan a meeting to discuss an issue or policy. The applicant uses his or her knowledge of the job and organization, experience with similar events, and expertise, and is evaluated on the basis of his or her responses and the priorities with which the items in the basket are approached. In general, work samples are beneficial as components of a selection program because they provide the employer with information about how the applicant might perform actual job tasks and they provide the applicants with a more realistic view of the job that they have applied for.

Assessment Centers

This last selection tool, assessment centers, is often used for hiring, as well as placement decisions and promotions within an organization. In an assessment center 10 or 12 applicants are simultaneously observed and evaluated by a group of judges. The evaluation will typically be based on a series of group and individual activities and tests. For example, applicants coming to an assessment center might first take a personality test and a general cognitive ability test. In addition, they may participate in both group and individual interviews, role plays, and other activities which reflect the contents of the job that they are applying for.

One popular activity in an assessment center is the leaderless group discussion in which the applicants are given a problem to discuss and are observed while they address this problem. During this activity the judges can assess the applicants' communication skills, problem-solving abilities, and their abilities to deal with stress and conflict. Individuals in an assessment center may also be evaluated by their peers (the other applicants) as well as by the center's judges. Each applicant will be rated on a series of dimensions such as decision-making ability, communication skills, flexibility, and motivation based on his or her performance on the tests and activities. Assessment centers are considered useful components of a selection system because they are seen as valid by the applicants and assessment center ratings do predict career progression and success in a variety of jobs. One of the drawbacks to this selection tool is the high cost: these centers usually require separate facilities, they employ a variety of people to function as evaluators, and the assessment typically takes place over two or three days.

Legal Issues in Selection and Other Employment Decisions

Equal Employment Opportunity

Since 1964, a number of government regulations have been enacted that apply to the selection process. I/O psychologists must address these issues in the development, implementation, and evaluation of a selection program. These regulations dictate which variables (and the measures used to collect these data) can be considered during selection and other employment decisions such as promotions and terminations. For example, the Age Discrimination in Employment Act prohibits employers from considering an applicant's age unless they can demonstrate that it is necessary for performing the job successfully. These laws also determine how employers must demonstrate that the measures used in selection or promotion are valid and job related.

Overall, these regulations were enacted to address concerns about fairness, discrimination, and bias in various personnel decisions including selection. Together, these laws and regulations aim to insure that all U.S. citizens have an equal opportunity to compete for and maintain jobs for which they are qualified, and that they have an equal opportunity for personal and economic independence. Table 2 highlights some of this legislation and outlines the central elements of those laws. In addition, one of those laws, the Americans with Disabilities Act of 1989 (ADA), is described in greater depth later in this section.

Equal employment opportunity legislation and the courts' interpretations of those laws have changed frequently over the last 25 years. I/O psychologists must stay abreast of these regulations in order to protect individual employees and applicants as well as the organizations for which they work. I/O psychologists must work hard to insure that the recruitment and selection procedures

51

they use are not biased against individuals on the basis of group membership. This means carefully evaluating tests, interviews, and all other measures used in selection to make sure that they do not have an adverse impact on a group of individuals. **Adverse impact** has occurred when the selection rates for individuals in different groups are substantially different. For example, if 70% of male applicants score above the cutoff on a simulation while only 45% of the female applicants have acceptable scores, the simulation has adverse impact on women. Typically, the **eighty percent rule** is applied to identify adverse impact. According to this rule, the percentage of majority applicants that have acceptable scores is calculated. The percentage of minority applicants is compared and should be no less than 4/5ths (80%) of the percentage for the majority applicants. In the above example 70% of the male applicants were successful on the simulation. Four fifths, (80%) of 70% would be 56%. Since less than 56% of the female applicants are successful on the simulation, the measure has adverse impact. If adverse impact is found, the employer can take at least two actions. First, the organization can demonstrate through a thorough job analysis and validity studies that the qualities measured during selection are job related. If this is true the organization must also show that there are no other measures of these qualities with similar validity that do not have adverse impact. Second, the employer could choose or develop another measure of the same skills which does not have adverse impact (Guion, 1991).

What happens when an employee believes that there has been a violation of these laws and regulations? First, the employee files a complaint with the EEOC (Equal Employment Opportunity Commission) or a state fair employment commission. This organization will then conduct an investigation and determine

Table 2
Equal Employment Opportunity Legislation

Legislation	Purpose
Equal Pay Act of 1968	Prohibits sex discrimination in pay for jobs requiring the same skill, effort, and working conditions
Civil Rights Act of 1964 (Amended 1991)	Prohibits using race, color, religion, sex, or national origin as a basis for employment decisions or privileges including selection, termination, working conditions, employment privileges, and training
Age Discrimination in Employment Act of 1967	Prohibits employment discrimination against individuals over age 40 unless the employer can demonstrate that age is a true occupational qualification
Americans with Disabilities Act of 1989	Prohibits employment discrimination against qualified applicants with current disabilities, a history of disability, or presumed disability. Also requires employers to make reasonable accommodations for employees with disabilities.

whether or not it is likely that discrimination did occur. If the EEOC finds reason to believe that a violation has occurred, they will try to resolve the dispute between the organization and employee through negotiation. If negotiation is not successful, the EEOC may file a lawsuit against the organization on behalf of the employee. I/O psychologists working for the employer may be asked to demonstrate through validity studies and other research that a selection program or employment decision is not discriminatory.

Affirmative Action Programs
In addition to ensuring that their employment practices are not discriminatory, employers may also make efforts to reduce the negative effects of past discrimination and barriers to employment. Affirmative action includes all programs initiated by an organization to compensate for the damage done by previous discriminatory practices. Actively recruiting individuals from under-represented groups, training managers and supervisors to eliminate prejudice and to promote all employees, or changing policies that might discourage members of under-represented groups from applying for a job, are examples of affirmative action programs. It is important to recognize that neither equal employment opportunity legislation nor affirmative action programs establish quotas or require organizations to hire unqualified applicants.

Unfortunately, I/O psychologists have observed that equal employment opportunity regulations and affirmative action guidelines are frequently misinterpreted and may evoke strong negative reactions. For example, Saal and Moore (1993) found that when considering equally qualified applicants, individuals perceived the promotion of a same sex applicant over an opposite sex applicant to be fair, while the promotion of the opposite sex applicant over the same sex applicant was not seen as fair. The researchers suggest that self-interest guided people's reactions to these scenarios. Men perceived the promotion of a male candidate as fair and women viewed the promotion of a female candidate as fair. In similar research done by Heilman, Block, and Lucas (1992) equally qualified female applicants who were identified as affirmative action hirees were considered less competent, less likely to advance, and were less well liked by their colleagues. These findings suggest that there are grave consequences for both individuals and organizations when employment decisions are not perceived as fair. The individuals may be less committed to the organization and have more negative attitudes. In addition, negative stereotypes may be applied to individuals who are perceived as receiving preferential treatment.

The Americans With Disabilities Act of 1990

The Americans with Disabilities Act of 1990 (ADA) was enacted to protect individuals with various disabilities or those who care for individuals with disabilities from discrimination by employers. This legislation prohibits employers from discriminating against **qualified job applicants with disabilities** and those who may have a relationship with a disabled individual. Qualified individuals with disabilities include those individuals who meet the job-related requirements such as education or experience and can perform the **essential functions** of the job *with or without* **reasonable accommodation**. The law covers individuals who have physical disabilities such as impaired vision or mobility, those with learning disabilities such as dyslexia, individuals with a severely limiting condition (or history of such a condition) such as cancer, mental illness, or drug abuse, individuals who are perceived as being substantially limited but who are not actually disabled such as those with obvious scars, and individuals who are HIV positive. Parents of disabled children, partners of disabled adults, or someone caring for an individual with a serious illness are also protected by this legislation. For example, it is illegal to not hire someone because of a fear that he or she will miss work while caring for a sick child or other relative, or that the individual's health insurance benefits will be too costly for the employer.

In the hiring process, determining if the disabled individual is qualified occurs in two phases. First, the employer must decide if the individual meets the job requirements specified through the job analysis. For example, does the applicant for a newspaper journalist's job have the necessary writing skills, or does an applicant for a nursing position have the appropriate education and certification? The measures used to make this decision must be valid for the disabled applicant. A test may need to be read for a sight-impaired applicant or an interpreter provided for an interview with a hearing impaired applicant. Second, the employer must establish whether or not the disabled individual can perform the essential job functions *with* or *without* reasonable accommodation. Essential functions represent the primary responsibilities of the job holder as determined through current practice, job descriptions and anticipated consequences for not doing the task.

Reasonable accommodation can include changes to the job such as delegating a minor responsibility to another individual, or adjusting the schedule so the employee could receive needed medical treatment. Reasonable accommodation may also involve altering the work environment by installing alarm systems for the hearing impaired, widening the entrance to an office, or making the line in the cafeteria wheelchair accessible. Finally, reasonable accommodation may require modifying current organizational practices such as allowing guide-dogs on the worksite or providing reserved parking spaces for physically handicapped individuals, which would afford equal employment opportunity to the disabled individual. Reasonable accommodation is only required for disabled individuals (not those who have a relationship with a disabled person). In addition, employers are not required to make accommodations that will place **undue**

hardship on the organization such as very expensive changes or those that substantially alter the way in which they conduct business.

Section Summary

Recruitment and selection is the process through which the organization attempts to maintain or expand an effective workforce by attracting qualified applicants and choosing those who are most likely to perform the job successfully. The first step in this process is to identify the needs of the organization as a whole and to clearly define the demands of the jobs to be filled. Job demands and requirements are identified through a set of procedures called job analysis. Job analyses are conducted using interviews and questionnaires, observing employees while they do their work or having job analysts perform some of the work tasks. In addition, this information about the job demands should be gathered from a variety of sources including job incumbents, supervisors, and clients. The results of the job analysis are used to choose appropriate measures for selection. The tools chosen to identify the most qualified applicants must be both reliable and valid. Most selection systems include a combination of measures including interviews, cognitive ability tests, personality tests, honesty tests, and work samples. The scores on these measures are combined to make the decision about the most qualified applicants for the position.

The procedures used in selection and other employment decisions are governed by a variety of regulations that mandate equal employment opportunity for all U.S. citizens. These regulations are designed to ensure that all individuals have an equal opportunity to compete for jobs for which they are qualified and include the Civil Rights Act of 1964 (as amended in 1991) and the Americans with Disabilities Act. I/O psychologists must stay informed about the most recent regulations to insure that the tests

that they develop and the methods that they use are in accordance
with these guidelines.

Training: Helping Employees Learn How to Perform Their Jobs

Once applicants have been hired to fill the jobs within an organization, the employer frequently needs to facilitate the effective performance of the job duties through training. Training is designed to teach employees about the elements of their jobs that they cannot perform when they are hired. It may also be used to improve the skills of employees who have been performing a job for some time especially when technology used on the job has changed or when the conditions under which the work is performed have been altered.

What is Training? When and Why is it Needed?

Organizations in the United States spend over 200 million dollars on training each year (Carnevale, Gainer, and Villet, 1990). Most training is relatively informal such as mentoring relationships, special assignments, or observing others on the job. Other training programs are much more structured, including seminars, college coursework, or elaborate training facilities. Training involves employees acquiring skills, knowledge, or attitudes in order to improve their work performance (Goldstein and Gilliam, 1990). When they are exposed to training, employees are learning new skills, mastering new work techniques, or acquiring information that they can use on their jobs. When developing training programs, I/O psychologists apply many of the principles that you may have studied earlier in this course in units about learning and conditioning, memory, and cognitive processes.

Training is used to meet a variety of individual and organizational needs. First, as the above definition suggests, training can be used to improve job performance. For example, an organization which

59

manufactures small appliances might introduce a training program to reduce the number of errors made during the assembly process. The program might teach employees how to detect flaws in the materials or identify appliances that have been incorrectly assembled before they are shipped to customers.

Training can also be an important part of career development, making an individual more likely to be promoted or be better prepared for future assignments. A company might assign a manager to a special joint task force for union representatives and management in order to give her experience in employee relations. This cooperative experience will be valuable if she is promoted to a plant manager's position. Similarly, training can be used to provide individuals with the skills needed to get a job. An organization closing a plant or laying-off a large number of employees may hold a seminar on resume writing or interview strategies in order to help those individuals find employment after the layoff. Training can be used to facilitate more effective relationships between an organization and the surrounding community. Cross-cultural training is used to facilitate adjustment for employees working outside their own countries. These trainees may learn about regional customs and business practices that will allow them to work and live comfortably in that culture.

Training can also be used to familiarize workers with technological change such as a new computer system or new piece of heavy equipment. This type of training may be scheduled frequently in some organizations because of rapid technological change. Training may also be used to improve interpersonal skills. A department store might design a training program to teach its store employees how to successfully handle customer complaints. Training has also been used to create a better working environment by teaching safer work practices, discussing sexual harassment or racial discrimination, and promoting teamwork or cooperation. Because training represents an opportunity for employees and an employment decision, it is also covered by the equal employment opportunity legislation discussed in the previous section. All employees should have an equal opportunity to be considered for training.

Goldstein (1986) developed a set of guidelines designed to ensure that training meets the needs of both individual employees and their organizations. He has developed a model which specifies three distinct steps in the development and introduction of a training program. His model suggests that these three steps form a feedback loop, a relationship in which the results and outcomes from each step are used to modify the procedures or contents of each step in the training process. Figure 3 outlines the essential steps in the training process as described by Goldstein (1986).

Needs Assessment: Who Needs to Learn What?

The first step in Goldstein's (1986) model is needs assessment: determining what the training program should accomplish for employees and employers. The needs analysis should identify the essential aspects of good performance and determine which of these will benefit from training (Campbell, 1988). Needs assessment typically includes three major components: organizational analysis, task analysis, and person analysis.

Organizational Analysis
During **organizational analysis**, the short and long term goals of the organization are examined and a set of parallel training goals are established (Latham, 1988). A department store may want to increase customer satisfaction by handling returns and exchanges more efficiently. An organization laying off a large number of employees wants to maintain a good relationship with the community and promote an image that is consistent with that

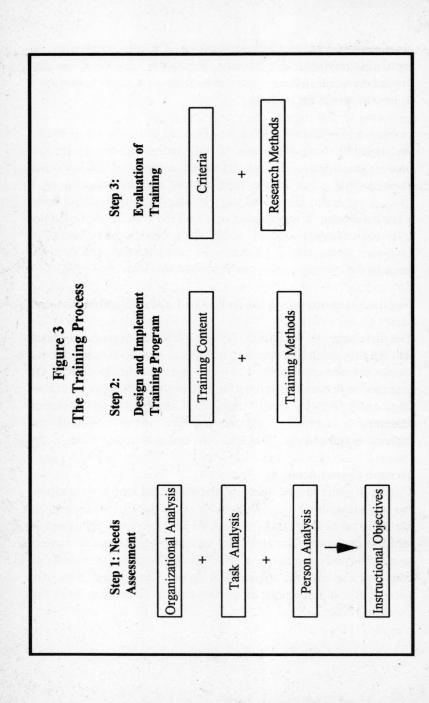

Figure 3
The Training Process

Step 1: Needs
Assessment

Organizational Analysis

+

Task Analysis

+

Person Analysis

→ Instructional Objectives

Step 2:
Design and Implement
Training Program

Training Content

+

Training Methods

Step 3:
Evaluation of
Training

Criteria

+

Research Methods

practice. A second aspect of organizational analysis focuses on evaluating organizational climate and support. How does training fit into the work environment? This analysis should determine the degree to which the training program is compatible with other programs within the organization such as selection, performance evaluation, and work rules or standards. This analysis should also consider the extent to which newly trained employees will receive support and encouragement from their managers, peers, and clients.

Task Analysis

The second aspect of needs assessment is **task analysis**. Task analysis generally begins with a thorough job analysis as described in the section about selection. This analysis will identify the essential activities that trainees will perform after training is complete. The job specifications, knowledge, skills, abilities and other characteristics (KSAOs) needed for success are also clarified during this process. The list of KSAOs may be separated into KSAOs needed to master the training objectives, KSAOs that should develop during the training program, and those KSAOs that can be learned after training is complete. To the extent that jobs require higher level cognitive skills such as abstract reasoning, complex problem solving, creative processes, or decision making, the task analysis will need to also focus on the learning processes or cognitive strategies that may be required of trainees (Tannenbaum and Yukl, 1992).

Person Analysis

The third step in the needs assessment process is **person analysis**. Determining who needs to be trained and identifying their pretraining characteristics or level of preparation. This analysis describes the current skills and abilities of those who are to be trained. For example, employees may need to review basic math concepts before learning to use a new internal accounting program. This process might also include determining if older and younger workers will benefit from different training methods, or evaluating the interest level of the trainees. For example, Bernick, Kindley, and Pettit (1984) found that managers at different levels of the organization reported different training needs. First line supervisors requested training for the technical aspects of their jobs such as writing memos and reports. Middle level managers requested human resources training to enhance their leadership skills or evaluate performance more effectively. Upper level managers indicated that they would benefit from training in conceptual processes such as goal setting and long range planning. In another study, Tucker (1985) found that middle-aged employees (40-49 years old) requested management training while those who were slightly older wanted training in new technologies. One of the concerns that researchers have about needs assessment is that in practice, self-report measures which only focus on what individual employees want are used to determine the training needs. Unfortunately, these measures do not necessarily assess what the organization needs from those employees.

The final step in the needs assessment process is writing a clear set of instructional objectives to describe what employees should be able to do after they have completed training. These objectives should describe a set of behaviors and other observable outcomes, the level of performance which indicates mastery of the assigned tasks, and the conditions under which they should be demonstrated. For example, when training employees who will be laid off how to search for and successfully apply for a job, the training objectives might include:

To write a cover letter in a standard business format which accurately reflects personal strengths and qualifications.

To identify five useful resources for information about job opportunities.

Training Design and Implementation

Characteristics of a Good Learning Experience

Once the instructional objectives have been specified, the training program can be developed and implemented; this is the second step in Goldstein's (1986) model. This step involves choosing both the content and methods of training. Training content grows out of the behavioral objectives specified during the needs analysis. It reflects the knowledge or skills trainees must master in order to perform their jobs (Campbell, 1988). The sequence in which these skills must be mastered should also be identified during this process. For example, trainees may need to learn how to operate new computer equipment and software before they can learn how to generate a report and summary of their weekly activities.

Once the necessary training content has been identified, the training methods are chosen. Researchers have attempted to identify the procedures which most effectively promote learning in trainees but as yet have not identified the methods which are consistently most effective. Sterns and Doverspike (1989) have suggested a set of guidelines for successful training that were initially developed for training older workers; they apply to other trainees as well.

1. Training should emphasize material that is job relevant and that builds self-confidence through positive feedback. Employees should be learning things that will improve their job performance in some way and they should receive frequent information about their progress.

2. Training should be designed so that trainees master one component completely before moving on to newer skills or tasks. If employees are still having difficulty performing the

earlier tasks, they will not be able to focus on mastering the later ones.

3. Training should, when possible, build on the prior knowledge and experience of the trainee. This practice can help employees learn material more effectively by connecting it to personal experience and by providing positive feedback.

4. The training program should not require a lot of memorization. Memorizing facts, figures, or procedures is rarely required on the job.

5. Trainees should not have to respond under time pressure unless it is essential for learning and performing the task. Again, allowing trainees plenty of time to perform the required tasks facilitates the positive feedback by allowing them to successfully complete the newly learned activities.

Other research suggests that learners should be required to actively participate in their learning and demonstrate their understanding through practice rather than observing others or listening to lectures (Campbell, 1988). Asking the trainees to produce the necessary responses in practice exercises, and applying them in different settings will enhance both initial learning and ultimate retention of the material. For example, the employees participating in a cross-cultural training course might role play a business luncheon or practice a telephone conversation with a client. Practice on these tasks will ensure that the employee can successfully communicate with individuals in the host culture and show respect for local traditions and practices. Research also suggests that teaching trainees metacognition and mnemonics can help them learn, especially when they are being taught tasks that will require complex cognitive processing (Cassidy-Schmitt & Newby, 1986; Hogan, Hakel, and Decker, 1986). Metacognition involves understanding, identifying and choosing appropriate strategies for learning and remembering. Through metacognition trainees learn to think about the learning process and to periodically evaluate both what they know and what they don't know. These authors suggest that trainees can learn to evaluate and compare their own cognitive abilities with those required to learn the material; trainees can then select appropriate learning strategies and modify them when necessary. You may remember a discussion of mnemonics from your study of memory. These tools can be used to facilitate memory of important information.

Finally, the training process is most effective when the learners are given plenty of **feedback**. Trainees need to know how well they are performing and when they have shown improvement. Campbell (1988) distinguishes between internal and external sources of feedback. Internal feedback is experienced within the trainee while external feedback is information gathered from events or sources that are separate from the employee. Learners responding to internal feedback may know their performance felt right or that they believe that they understand the new concepts. External feedback can be either primary or secondary. An employee receiving primary external feedback might see that the product works when tested while an individual gathering secondary external feedback might be told by the boss that the report was well done. In order for feedback to enhance learning it should be positive whenever possible. Telling employees how their performance has improved is more useful and encouraging than pointing out only their mistakes. This positive feedback must also be perceived as sincere and accurate. The source should be perceived as knowledgeable and fair. In addition, feedback should be specific, connected to the instructional objectives, and unaffected by intervening events such as someone else's opinion or poor performance. Vague feedback such as "You are doing better," or information that compares an individual's performance to that of others is not as useful to the trainee as more specific and objective information.

While there are a few general guidelines for designing effective training, training developers need to consider a variety of factors and conditions when designing a training program. The nature of the skills and knowledge to be learned, the prior knowledge, abilities, attitudes and beliefs of the trainees, and the context in which the tasks will be learned and practiced can all affect training success. Organizations must know: Do the employees believe that training will help them to perform better? For example, the department store employees who do not expect that training will help them to handle disgruntled customers more effectively are unlikely to be interested in the training course. Will the employees receive some benefit from performing their jobs better? If the department store employees do not believe that supervisors will reward them for having fewer customer complaints, then they are unlikely to be motivated to learn. Do the employees believe that they can successfully complete training and master its content? If the employees believe the computers are just too complicated for them to understand, they will not be interested in a training program designed to teach them how to use the computers (Campbell, 1988; Noe, 1986).

Self-efficacy reflects trainees' beliefs that they can successfully learn what is being taught in training. High self-efficacy facilitates both performance on tests after training and later using what has been learned in the work environment (Gist, Schoerer, and Rosen, 1989). One way to build efficacy during the training process is to begin with simple tasks and behaviors that can be mastered easily and then progress to more complex behaviors as trainees become more confident. This process may be combined with goal setting; the individual adopts difficult but attainable subgoals. Success with those goals provides clear feedback on progress and enhances self-efficacy. Efficacy can also be increased by using extrinsic reinforcement, rewarding employees for improved performance. The individuals then gradually develop a value for the type of performance required and may often gain some social rewards for their efforts. In general, self-efficacy will increase when the individual continues to experience mastery in situations that were originally viewed as threatening and when his or her fears about the difficulty of the task are disconfirmed (Bandura, 1982, 1986). In contrast, the training process should be designed to avoid unfamiliar or surprising events which might emphasize the individual's inexperience or limited skills and therefore reduce self-efficacy.

Efficacy for mastering knowledge or skills may also be affected by whether an individual believes the abilities needed to perform them are fixed or malleable. Those trainees who believe that their abilities are fixed (not affected by practice or experience) are most likely to set performance outcome goals, identifying a specific level of performance that he or she expects to achieve or setting a standard of performance. For example, a sales trainee believing that sales skills are fixed or unchangeable might set a goal of making a sale on 50 percent of his sales calls. In contrast, those trainees who believe that abilities change with time and experience are likely to set learning goals - setting a standard of improvement or growth. These trainees are more likely to set a goal of improving sales by 2% each month. While the individuals in the first group may initially set higher goals for performance, the employees in the second group will continue to work toward higher levels of performance and will eventually set goals that are higher than those for the first group. These individuals are also likely to respond differently when they have low efficacy for a task. The employee who considers these abilities fixed is likely to avoid trying the task because he does not anticipate success, while the individual who believes that abilities can change will be more likely to attempt the task and to persist because improvement is expected (Campbell, 1988).

In addition to understanding how trainees view their abilities, I/O psychologists choosing training methods should adapt to the measured level of ability and the prior knowledge of the trainees. Research by Snow and Lohman (1984) suggests that a relatively unstructured and complex learning environment is best for high ability learners while a tightly structured and simplified environment is most useful to low ability learners. Other researchers suggest that training success is a function of both ability and motivation; trainees must have both the skills and the desire to do the assigned work (Tannenbaum & Yukl, 1992). To summarize, it appears that training is most successful when the programs are designed to accommodate the abilities of the trainees, when training works to enhance trainees' self-efficacy or expectations of success, and when trainees are motivated to perform the new tasks successfully.

Training Methods and Techniques
Many different training methods have been developed that consider the issues raised above. These training methods have been successful under different circumstances but more research is needed to determine which methods are optimal under particular conditions. Because of this uncertainty, I/O psychologists have begun to combine training methods into packages. This approach allows psychologists to combine the most effective training techniques when teaching a variety of tasks and may be more realistic than trying to sort out the specific circumstances under which each method is effective (Latham, 1989).

One popular method for training managers is mentoring. Many companies rely on informal mentoring programs in which more advanced managers develop a strong relationship with a newer employee. Noe (1988) reports that mentoring serves two main functions. First, the psychosocial function includes acceptance, encouragement, coaching and counseling. A mentor might review and make suggestions on reports or presentations, or suggest effective ways of dealing with a difficult supervisor. The career facilitation function includes sponsorship, protection, challenging assignments, exposure, and visibility. Mentors will suggest that the newer employee be given a task force assignment or may intervene when another manager is angry about a mistake. One problem with informal mentoring systems is that the employees who might need the training the most are often the least likely to receive the help. If instead, companies use a formal, assigned, mentoring program, not all the mentors will provide the support and career development that is important because they may be less committed to the program or less interested in the mentee.

A second form of training that is getting increased attention is team-oriented training. With the increased focus on teamwork, training programs need to adapt to those different needs by using team training or team building. Team training involves establishing specific learning objectives including skills, knowledge, and attitudes for members of the team while they learn as a group. One problem with team training is that most measures of performance that might be used in the evaluation stage are at the individual level and are not easily adapted into a group measure. Team building is designed to help individuals and teams develop behaviors and good relationships by teaching team members to practice mutual performance monitoring and feedback exchange, communication and coordination of activities.

Technology has also played a major role in the development of training methods. Computer aided instruction (CAI) allows large numbers of individuals to participate in the same training program simultaneously while working at a comfortable pace. In this form of training, the employee works through modules or lessons on the computer and is able to get immediate feedback, to actively practice the material learned, to diagnose problems or difficulties, and to get remedial help when needed. The primary drawback to

CAI is the time and money needed to develop the complex software used in these programs.

A second training technology that has become more popular is the use of interactive videodiscs. The videodisc can show material in a variety of forms including still photographs, clips from videotapes or films, computer graphics, text and audio recordings. In their simplest form videodiscs allow learners to choose which information they will work with; more complex systems allow the individual to interact with the material, practice what he or she has learned and get feedback on his or her performance. Finally, technology has also allowed organizations to expand their training opportunities geographically. By introducing teleconferencing, using satellite television and other long-distance media, organizations can effectively provide training to individuals who are separated geographically without having to spend a lot of money on travel and other expenses.

Transfer: Using What Has Been Learned

While it is important that the trainee master the material presented in the training program, organizations are equally interested that the knowledge, skills, and attitudes be successfully applied when the employee returns to the actual work setting. Baldwin and Ford (1988) identify two components of transfer: generalization and maintenance. **Generalization** occurs when employees use skills they learned when they return from training, and maintenance occurs when employees continue to use the new knowledge and skills in the work setting after a significant period of time has elapsed since training. A number of factors influence the extent to which this transfer from training environment to work environment occurs. First, supervisory support appears to be essential in the transfer process. Supportive supervisors have employees who enter training with greater interest and motivation because they believe that it will be useful when they return (Cohen, 1990). This support can be conveyed by establishing goals prior to training, giving employees time to prepare for training, and providing encouragement.

After the training program has been completed, supervisors can provide recently trained employees with reinforcement for newly learned skills, modeling of appropriate behaviors, and goal-setting to facilitate the **maintenance** of trained behaviors. It appears then that supportive supervisors establish circumstances that both promote more effective learning of the material and make the use of newly learned skills more likely once employees return to their jobs. In addition to support, Baldwin and Magjuka (1991) found that if employees expect that there will be some follow-up or assessment once they return to the work setting they are more focused on transfer to the real work environment. These activities suggest to trainees that they are responsible for their own learning and that it will be important for their success on the job. Unfortunately, elements of the work environment can also inhibit transfer once the employee returns. Ridicule from peers, inadequate equipment and resources or highly constrained work environments discourage or prohibit employees from using their new knowledge and skills (Tannenbaum & Yukl, 1992).

Evaluation: Did the Training Have the Expected Effects?

After training has been completed, the third step in Goldstein's model, **training evaluation** is initiated. Organizations need to know both if individuals have learned what they should have learned and if the training program has been effective in meeting the organization's goals.

Selecting the Criteria for Success
The first step in the evaluation process is to select appropriate criteria for success. Kirkpatrick (1976) identifies four types of criteria that should be assessed after training: employee reactions

to the training, learning of knowledge, skills, and attitudes, performance of those skills after training, and organizational results. The first three of these criteria reflect the instructional objectives and can be measured at the individual level soon after training. How do employees feel about the training program? Do they believe that they have learned useful skills? Have employees learned the content covered during training? Are employees using their new skills on the job? The last criterion, organizational results, will need to be measured more broadly and may occur long after training has been completed. The organization may want to know if the performance changes that result from the training program have reduced costs, turnover, accidents or grievances or met other organizational goals. These outcomes provide some of the best reasons for continuing a training program or making changes to it. Managers will take training more seriously if there is visible improvement in employee behavior and achievement of organizational objectives (Latham, 1988).

Choosing the Research Method

The process of training evaluation is a specific example of psychological research. The methods used are founded in the principles of the scientific method and the techniques used throughout the discipline of psychology that you have studied during this course. Once the criteria for training success have been selected, a training evaluation model is chosen. Research designed to evaluate training is often difficult to conduct and interpret. There may not be an appropriate control group or the benefits of training may appear only after a substantial amount of time has passed.

The evaluation model which is appropriate depends on the questions to be answered. When the organization wants to know if training has benefitted the individual trainees or parts of the organization, a **summative evaluation** should be conducted.

Summative evaluations typically involve comparing a trained group with an untrained control group. If the training is effective, the trained group should perform at a higher level than the untrained group. For example, if a hospital has initiated a program to reduce the incidence of hepatitis B among its staff, the group of employees which has been trained should have fewer cases of the disease than the group which has not been trained. Even if there is not an appropriate control group (in this example there may be ethical concerns about not training everyone) the rate of infection after the program was introduced could be compared to the same measure taken prior to training. If training has been useful, the rate of infection should be lower after training. Studies of this type generally use broad rather than specific performance measures to determine training effectiveness and may therefore underestimate the value of training. If in the previous example, the hospital compares the number of sick days taken by employees before the training with that same statistic after the training there may not be a significant difference. The training was targeted at reducing the incidence of a particular disease, only one of many reasons that people might use their sick days.

A second evaluation model, **comparative summative evaluations** involve comparing the usefulness of two or more different training programs. This research design includes two treatment groups (training program A and training program B) and at least one untrained control group. For example, a department store chain has been using on-the-job training to teach employees how to use the computerized cash registers and inventory systems. The organization's human resource group has recently designed a four-hour seminar to teach this same material. Before offering the seminar at all stores across the country, the organization should compare the number of errors made by a group trained through the on-the-job technique (program A), a group which has taken the seminar (program B), and an untrained control group. If the seminar is a better training method, the employees who have completed this course should make significantly fewer errors than the other two groups.

The third evaluation model, **formative evaluation** is designed to detect what might have gone wrong in a training program and what aspects of the program could be improved. Frequently, this type of evaluation is informal and is based on employee reactions to the training program. Formative evaluations determine if the training methods are well matched to the training content, or measure trainees abilities and attitudes. A formative evaluation may also identify conflicts between the training program and other organizational practices.

Training the Unemployed

Various organizations have addressed the needs of the unemployed in order to have them participate in the workforce. One group of unemployed individuals of particular concern are the hard-core unemployed: individuals who have not been a regular members of the workforce or have not been employed during the last six months (Goldstein and Gilliam, 1990). To date, much work with members of this group has been unsuccessful, after training many are still unemployed. This may occur because the training program is poorly designed or implemented, because the skills expected are above the capabilities of these individuals. Training the hard core unemployed can also be difficult because they lack basic literacy and math skills, because they do not have some of the job search skills such as completing an application or participating in a interview or because the organization does not show any sort of commitment to the employee but instead expects that all the effort and change must come from the trainees.

Vinokur, van Ryn, Gramlich, and Price (1991) developed and tested the effects of a program designed to help unemployed individuals. These researchers took a dual approach to the problem of unemployment. First they focused on providing the resources and skills that facilitate re-employment and should reduce the amount of time that an individual is unemployed. How can we help unemployed people get jobs more readily? Second, the researchers tried to reduce the negative psychological and physical consequences that are often associated with unemployment.

Nearly 1000 unemployed individuals from Michigan participated in the study. The experimental group participated in eight three-hour sessions designed to enhance the job seeking confidence, increase the motivation to seek a job, and improve the mental health of the unemployed participants. The control group did not participate in this course. Participants were surveyed before the training, one month after the training, four months after the training, and 32 months after the training. At one month and four months after the intervention, those in the experimental group were working significantly more hours per week than those in the control group. At 32 months, the individuals who had participated in the sessions were making more money per hour than those who had not participated. The participants who had been in the control group also reported making fewer changes in employers and working more than 30 hours per week for a greater amount of time since the intervention. Finally, even those who participated in the intervention but who remained unemployed, showed fewer signs of depression and higher confidence and motivation for job seeking. These results suggest that training programs can be developed which will facilitate the re-entry of unemployed individuals into the workforce more quickly and with positive consequences for their economic independence and psychological well-being.

Section Summary

Training involves teaching employees new skills, knowledge, or procedures that can help them to perform their jobs. Training can be used to improve job performance, to provide career development, to familiarize workers with technological changes or to create a better work environment. Goldstein (1986) has developed a three-step model of the training process. The first step in this process is needs assessment: determining what the training program should accomplish for employee and employers. This step typically involves examining the organization, the job to be performed, and the people who will be performing the work in order to understand what the training program should accomplish. The second step in Goldstein's model is training design and implementation: determining what should be taught and how it should be taught to employees. In general, training methods should emphasize material that is job relevant and that can be mastered in a sequence of simpler tasks. Training should emphasize active participation, foster a sense of self-efficacy in the trainees, and provide them with frequent, positive feedback. Organizations are also concerned that the skills learned during the training program be applied once the employee returns to the actual work environment. This transfer of training is facilitated by support from supervisors, and realistic training conditions. Once the training is complete, organizations must also evaluate the effectiveness of the training program to determine if it has met the original objectives.

Motivation: Working Harder and Better

Assuming that an organization has an effective selection system in place that allows it to hire the most qualified applicants and that it has implemented a well-designed training program to ensure that employees have the skills needed to perform their jobs, what other factors facilitate effective performance from the employees? In this next section you will read about workplace motivation: the factors that direct the level of effort that employees put toward accomplishing a task.

What is Motivation and Why is it Important?

You may have studied motivation earlier during this course. If so, you probably studied phenomena such as hunger, thirst, and sexual behavior. With the knowledge about these processes as a foundation, I/O psychologists study motivation as it applies to work. In addition, these researchers and practitioners have used this understanding to enhance the motivation of employees in the workplace. Although specific definitions are rarely agreed on, motivation is typically viewed as having three distinct effects on individuals.

1. **Motivation plays a role in initiating or directing performance of a task.** Research on motivation attempts to understand why people choose to perform some tasks and not others and practitioners try to encourage employees to focus on some work tasks and behaviors over others. For example, if a department store wants to promote customer satisfaction, it may reward employees who make extra efforts to meet customers' needs. These employees can call other stores in the region to look for items that are out of stock, process returns without hassles and questions, or write notes to customers to thank them for their business or tell them about a sale.

2. **Motivation determines the level of effort applied to performing a task.** Research in workplace motivation attempts to understand why some individuals will try harder than others. For example, an I/O psychologist might conduct research to understand why one plant makes more effort to reach its monthly production quota than a second plant. Practitioners might attempt to provide incentives such as bonuses or recognition which will facilitate greater levels of effort in the second plant.

3. **Motivation affects whether or not performance of a task is sustained** (Campbell & Pritchard, 1976; Kanfer, 1990; Komaki, Coombs & Schepman, 1991). Research in motivation attempts to understand why some employees will continue working hard at a task when others will not. For example, a researcher might design a study to understand how motivation affects persistence on a task in the presence of failure or frustration. An I/O psychologist might suggest that a company allow employees to perform a variety of tasks during the day so that they remain interested in all of them, provide regular incentives such as monthly prizes or bonuses, or identify an "employee of the month" in an attempt to maintain consistent levels of performance.

In general, research on motivation and motivational programs developed by practitioners should enhance the productivity of individuals, work groups, and organizations as a whole. Improving productivity means using fewer resources such as time, energy, raw materials, or employees to produce the same product or services (Campbell & Campbell, 1988; Mahoney, 1988). Increased productivity has a number of benefits both for the organization and the individual employee. With more productive employees, the organization is able to accomplish its goals more efficiently: perhaps the tasks are completed in less time and it costs the organization less money to complete the work, or increased efficiency can mean a reduction of costly errors or mistakes. The individual can benefit from the increased productivity if the organization shares those gains with employees through increased wages or stable, long term employment.

Theories of Motivation

Research has been conducted on many aspects of work motivation and a variety of theories have been developed to describe and understand the processes and results of workplace motivation. Early research and theories in the field of I/O psychology focused on the functions of physiological arousal, incentives, and drives on work behavior. Later work investigated the role of cognitive processes such as personal expectations about performance and rewards and decision-making on performance. More recent efforts have focused on goals set by supervisors or employees and self-regulation as components of motivation as well as personality and individual difference variables such as needs for personal growth and development (Kanfer, 1990).

Katzell and Thompson (1990) classify motivational theories into two separate categories: exogenous theories and endogenous theories. **Exogenous theories of motivation** focus on the factors that can be used and manipulated by the organization to modify an individual's work behavior. These theories examine the role of individual needs and values, of various incentives and rewards, and of goals in determining the level of effort that an individual puts toward his or her work. In contrast, **endogenous theories of motivation** focus on the cognitive processes used by the individual to interpret incentives and rewards, or evaluate elements of the work environment. While the organization can change an individual's pay or provide recognition for good work, endogenous theories emphasize that this change has no direct effects on how the employee views and organizes his or her understanding of the work environment. These theories discuss the role of social comparisons between employees, expectations of success or failure, and the perceived value of a reward to an individual. These individual interpretations can affect the level of effort that an employee will put toward organizational goals or determine whether employees will continue to perform their jobs well. Endogenous and exogenous theories of motivation imply very different behavior on the part of the organization attempting to improve the performance of its employees. Exogenous theories suggest that organizations modify reward systems, incentives, or goals to enhance individual or group performance. In contrast, endogenous theories imply a more complex and uncertain path for organizations. They must understand how these reward systems, incentives, and goals will be interpreted by employees before making attempts to influence those interpretations and ultimately improving job performance.

Exogenous theories of motivation
Need theories of motivation:
One set of exogenous theories of motivation are **need theories**. According to these theories, individuals have a set of needs which energize and direct their behavior (Cherrington, 1989). These needs can be physical, psychological, or social and are typically described as internal states of deficiency or deprivation which direct a person's behavior. Individuals will typically take some form of action to restore the internal equilibrium or relieve the tension caused by the deprivation: they are motivated to satisfy the needs (Cherrington, 1989; Kanfer, 1990).

Research on need theories has attempted to understand the content of human needs. Some researchers have suggested that humans share a common set of needs, while others have proposed that each individual has a unique combination of needs. In addition, research on need theories has attempted to discover how needs direct or guide behavior toward performing certain tasks in the workplace. Need theories would suggest that organizations can direct employees' behavior by providing them with opportunities

82

to satisfy their needs in the workplace. If an employee has a need to have meaningful relationships with co-workers, the organization might encourage teamwork or promote social activities after work. If an employee has a need to experience a sense of accomplishment, the organization can provide clear feedback on progress toward a goal or advertise the positive effects that its products have on individuals who use or purchase them. If an employee needs to buy a new home or save for a child's college education, the organization can provide financial incentives such as a bonus program or a savings plan.

One of the most widely accepted need theories was developed by Abraham Maslow. Maslow (1943) suggests that humans have a set of common needs that exist in a hierarchy from basic, physiological needs to higher-order psychological needs. Maslow argues that individuals are motivated to take actions that will satisfy unmet needs. In addition, he hypothesized that lower order needs must be largely satisfied before higher order needs will direct behavior. In other words, individuals will perform in ways to move themselves through the hierarchy and satisfy increasingly higher level needs. This concept is known as the **satisfaction-progression principle**.

At the base of Maslow's hierarchy are the survival or **physiological needs**. This category includes the need for food, water, sleep, and sex. In the workplace these needs may be met in part through pay (it can be used to purchase a number of things which meet these basic needs), work schedules and the cafeteria. The second level of needs in Maslow's hierarchy is **safety and security needs**. This group includes the need for safety, protection, freedom from fear, and the need for order or structure in daily activities at work. These needs are addressed through safe working conditions, health and life insurance benefits, and assurances of job security. In the middle of Maslow's hierarchy are the **social needs**. This category includes needs for meaningful relationships with other individuals such as partners, children, and friends. This set of needs may be met through good relationships with co-workers, support and concern from supervisors, and professional associations. The fourth level of Maslow's hierarchy is **ego and esteem needs**. This category can be further divided into internally and externally focused needs. The internally focused needs emphasize what the employees can do to enhance their self-images or self-esteem and include achievement, mastery, confidence, and independence. These needs may be addressed in the workplace by giving employees work that allows them to have a sense of accomplishment, and by allowing them to make some of the decisions about how to do the work. The externally focused needs in this category focus on acknowledgment and recognition from other individuals and include needs for reputation, status, and appreciation from others. These needs can be addressed through job titles, public recognition of good work, and providing individuals with promotions into high status jobs. Finally, at the top of Maslow's hierarchy are the **self-actualization needs**. This category includes needs for continuous growth and self-development and a need to fulfill one's potential. These needs may be met in the workplace by opportunities to learn new skills and to use them once they have been mastered, through mentoring programs in which individuals are given guidance and help to develop their talents and strengthen their weaknesses. See Table 3 for more examples of Maslow's hierarchy.

While Maslow's model has been widely accepted by organizations there is less empirical evidence to support his theory. Much of the research suggests significant flaws in Maslow's theory. First, little of the research designed to test Maslow's theory has measured changes in individual employees' needs over time. In order to show that individuals progress through the hierarchy in the way specified by Maslow, research must be designed to observe those developments. Second, studies by Hall and

Table 3
Programs and Incentives Which Represent Maslow's Need Hierarchy

Self Actualization Needs: entrepreneurship programs within the company, training and career development programs, continuing education programs or tuition reimbursement policies.

Esteem Needs: Awards such as 'employee of the month', 'salesperson of the year', job titles, recognition from supervisors.

Social Needs: Team projects, picnics or sporting events sponsored by employers, working with clients, customers or students.

Safety/Security Needs: Safety training and standards, disability or life insurance programs, outplacement services for employees who are laid off, policies prohibiting harassment or discrimination, retirement plans.

Physiological Needs: wages and salaries, cafeteria, water fountains and drink machines.

Nougaim(1968) and Lawler and Suttle (1972) found a positive correlation between need satisfaction and need importance. The more a need has been satisfied, the more important it becomes to the employee. Maslow's theory predicts that as a need is satisfied, the needs at the next level in the hierarchy become more important. In other words, Maslow's theory implies that as a need has been largely satisfied it should become less important to the individual. Third, while the hierarchy is intuitively appealing, most research does not show evidence for five distinct categories of needs (Wanous & Zwany, 1977). Finally, unfulfilled needs do not typically get the individual's undivided attention. Instead, individuals may simultaneously put effort toward activities which will satisfy needs at different levels of the hierarchy. For example, a computer programmer may work to improve her performance in order to get a year-end bonus and at the same time make efforts to improve or maintain her relationships with co-workers.

Alderfer (1969) attempted to address some of these concerns in his modification of Maslow's theory labeled ERG theory. First, he created only three categories of needs: Existence (physiological and safety), Relatedness (social and the external esteem needs) and Growth (internal esteem and self-actualization). Second, Alderfer argues that the needs in the various categories can be sought simultaneously. Individuals do not have to completely satisfy the needs at one level before attempting to satisfy those in a different level. Third, Alderfer claims that individuals will move through the hierarchy in one of two different ways. Like Maslow, Alderfer suggests that an individual will move to the next higher level when the needs at the previous level have largely been met (satisfaction-progression). For example, a graphic artist may begin to focus on developing new skills and learning state-of-the-art techniques after receiving his promotion. In addition, ERG theory suggests that an individual may seek to satisfy lower order needs when his or her attempts to meet higher order needs are unsuccessful. This process is labeled **frustration-regression**. For example, if a salesperson is repeatedly turned down for a promotion, he may begin to ensure his job security or may become more interested in the specifics of his benefits package (Alderfer, 1969). Alderfer's theory has received less attention than Maslow's from researchers. While there is some support, particularly for the need categories, the process of moving through the hierarchy is still largely untested.

A third need theory was developed by McClelland. McClelland's work focused on three psychological motives which would be particularly relevant in the workplace: need for achievement, need for affiliation, and need for power. McClelland (1987) argues that these motives each represent a group of incentives which will all have similar effects on the individual.

Need for achievement is considered a predisposition to strive for success (Campbell & Pritchard, 1976). Individuals who are high in the need for achievement have a strong desire for accomplishment and excellence; they want to improve their performance for the sake of doing something better (McClelland, 1987). As employees, individuals with a high need for achievement are likely to be comfortable with high levels of responsibility. They prefer to work with co-workers who are competent rather than those whom they like. Individuals with high need for achievement are also likely to set moderately difficult goals and to want frequent feedback on their progress. Those employees who are high in need for achievement are likely to be innovative and may often be restless and more likely to cheat than those who are lower in this need. When money is given as a reward, employees high in need for achievement view it as a measure of success. They are motivated by money as a symbol of success. When time off from work is used as an incentive, these individuals perform less well than employees with lower levels of need for achievement. People who are high in need for achievement do not find time off as rewarding as other individuals.

The concept behind need for achievement has been used to encourage individuals to become economically independent and to spur economic development. Through training, individuals can develop a high need for achievement and have a better chance of success as entrepreneurs. Researchers taught groups of entrepreneurs from several cities in India how to think and act like individuals who are high in need for achievement; they were encouraged to think and behave more confidently, were taught to use goal setting, and to monitor their progress toward their goals.

Two years after this training was complete, the researchers found evidence for increased business activity in cities where the training had occurred (little change in activity was observed in cities without this training). Similarly, individual indices of business activity and success also increased significantly when the trainees were compared to those business people who had not received the need for achievement training (McClelland, 1987) .

The second of McClelland's needs, the **need for affiliation** represents the desire to develop and maintain friendly and warm relationships with others. Individuals who have a high need for affiliation are likely to desire the approval of others and may be prone to conform when they are pressured by those individuals whom they value or respect. People with high need for affiliation express a sincere interest in other's feelings and want to work with other people. These needs may be met through cohesive and supportive work groups and effective and supportive supervision.

The third need which McClelland and his colleagues focused on was need for power. Individuals who have a high **need for power** show a desire to control others and influence their behavior. As employees, these individuals want positions of influence where they can direct the activities of others and control the outcomes of their efforts. The maintenance of leader-follower relations is crucial to these individuals. Employees with a high need for power are likely to want to advance to positions of power and influence within the organization.

In addition to investigating the behaviors typical of people with these needs individually, McClelland and his colleagues have studied the behaviors of people with particular patterns of needs. Specifically, McClelland and Boyatzis (1982) identified the **leadership motive pattern**. This pattern of needs predicts the long-term success of top level managers in non-technical management jobs. Individuals who display the leadership motive pattern have moderate to high need for power, low need for affiliation, and high degrees of self-control. These individuals are interested in influencing the behavior of others, are able to make difficult decisions without being concerned about others' approval, and like to maintain the order within an organization.

Goal Theory:

Locke (1968) suggested that the intent to work toward a goal can be an effective motivating force for individuals and groups. Goal theory suggests that organizations can improve productivity by establishing clear and measurable performance goals for individual employees or work groups. A **goal** is what an individual or group is attempting to accomplish, it is the target outcome for an action (Locke, Shaw, Saari & Latham, 1981). Goals enhance performance by directing the employee's attention to desired tasks, by initiating effort on those tasks, increasing persistence, and encouraging the development of strategy for reaching those goals (Locke, Shaw, Saari & Latham, 1981). Research on this theory has identified several characteristics of successful goal setting.

1. **Goal setting is most likely to improve performance if the goals are specific.** For example, an organization might set a goal of reducing travel expenses by 5% within the next six months. Telling employees to do their best is typically not as effective for improving performance as specific goals are.

2. **The goals should be challenging.** Locke (as cited in Mitchell and Silver, 1990) has argued that the most effective goals are set so that individuals have a 10% chance of goal attainment. Though employees trying to meet difficult goals may frequently not reach them, they typically perform better than those employees working toward easier and more attainable goals (Locke, 1968).

3. **Employees should have the abilities and resources needed to attain the goals.** Goals can be motivating only if they are possible to attain.

4. **Employees should be given feedback which provides information about their progress toward the goal.** The feedback can act as reward for efforts made so far and can help the employee improve performance where possible.

5. **Rewards are given for goal attainment.** Employees who meet the goals should be recognized and rewarded for their efforts and success.

6. **Management needs to support and participate in the goal setting program.**

7. **Goal setting will be most effective if the employees accept the goals that have been set.** One way to facilitate acceptance is to have employees participate in the goal setting process (Pritchard, Roth, Jones, Galgay, and Watson, 1986).

Recent research on goal setting has focused on comparing the effectiveness of group goals and individual goals. Mitchell and Silver (1990) found that group performance on a task which required cooperation among individuals was best when both individual and group goals were set. In other words, the group must have a goal and each member should have goals which will contribute to the group's success. In addition, setting group goals seemed to facilitate the development of a cooperative work strategy among group members. When only individual goals were set, group members were more likely to act competitively.

Goal theory makes obvious recommendations to the organization trying to enhance the performance of individuals and work groups. Clear, difficult, performance goals should be set on a regular basis. Progress toward those goals should be monitored, and goal attainment should be rewarded. These activities are common practice within many organizations as you will discover in a later section on motivational programs.

Reinforcement theory:

Reinforcement theory is founded in the principles of operant conditioning that you probably remember from earlier in this course. This theory focuses on how the consequences that follow a behavior affect an individual's performance of that behavior. The consequences of an employee's behavior (something which occurs after the behavior, such as receiving recognition from the supervisor, or having pay docked for being late) act as motivators by affecting the probability that the behavior will occur again. You may remember the **Law of Effect** which states that behaviors followed by unpleasant consequences will be less likely to reoccur in the future, while those behaviors that are followed by pleasant consequences will be more likely to occur in the future.

Reinforcement theory has been shown to be effective in improving a variety of work behaviors including safety, customer relations and productivity (Komaki et al., 1991). The consequences used to shape behavior can include promotions, pay increases, opportunities to engage in preferred activities, social recognition, and feedback or information about performance. For example, if an insurance agency wants to reduce the errors of adjusters' reports it might implement a system in which for every 10 consecutive reports without an error that an adjuster submits, he or she receives an opportunity to win dinner for two at a nice, local restaurant.

When reinforcement theory is applied in the workplace, it is typically imposed in four steps:

1. The desired performance or behavior are specified by the organization from the job analysis and organizational goals.

2. The employees' progress toward that behavior is measured using the job performance criteria and the performance appraisal system.

3. The organization rearranges the consequences to guide the behavior in the desired direction by rewarding the desired behaviors and perhaps punishing the unwanted behaviors.

4. The effectiveness of this intervention is evaluated (Komaki, Coombs, & Schepman, 1991).

Reinforcement theory can also be used to explain why organizations often observe behaviors that do not meet organizational objectives (Kerr, 1987). For example, an organization tells division managers not to spend more than is in their current budgets. When new budgets are prepared the following year, the organization only cuts those budgets in which all the money was not spent and increases budgets for managers who spent more than was in their budgets. The organization has, in effect, rewarded those who spend all of the money and punished those who did what was asked of them. Given these consequences, managers are likely to disregard the request and spend all the money in their budgets.

Endogenous Theories of Motivation
Expectancy Theory:
The next set of motivational theories expand the concept of motivation beyond an individual's desire to seek certain outcomes. Expectancy theories, a set of endogenous motivational theories, suggest that an individual's behavior is a function of conscious choices among alternatives (Mitchell, 1974). These choices are

made after considering three variables: expectancies, instrumentalities and valences. An **expectancy** is a belief that effort will lead to a particular level of performance. A salesperson may expect that he will need to put in extra hours on weekends or evenings in order to meet his quarterly sales goal. **Instrumentality** reflects the perceived connection between that level of performance and particular outcomes. It is the probability that a certain level of performance will lead to other outcomes. This salesperson believes that if he meets this quarterly goal, he will receive recognition from his supervisor, a $500 bonus, and is more likely to be considered for a promotion to District Sales Manager. **Valence** describes the degree of preference for those outcomes; it is based on the individual's anticipated satisfaction from receiving them. This salesperson may want to purchase a new VCR with the bonus and is very interested in the management position. Because valence reflects the individual's anticipated and not actual satisfaction, expectancy theory does not directly depend on the benefits that people actually experience from these outcomes. This salesperson may later get promoted to the District Manager's position and find he does not like his new job responsibilities.

Expectancy theory can be summarized by three questions: Expectancy is represented by the question "Can I perform this task successfully if I try?". Instrumentality is represented by the question "If I perform the task, what are the consequences or outcomes that will follow?". Valence is represented by the question "Do I value the outcome(s) that I will receive?". Together, these questions suggest that individuals will choose to perform at the levels that they believe will maximize their overall best interest. They will put effort toward the tasks on which they expect success and anticipate receiving desirable rewards for their performance. Most versions of expectancy theory include a series of mathematical equations to express the proposed relationships between these three components. Much of the research about expectancy theory has focused on these equations and the specifics of the relationships between expectancies, instrumentalities and valence (Mitchell, 1974; Kanfer, 1990).

Expectancy theory implies specific actions for organizations to take in order to motivate their employees.

1. Supervisors should make sure that people are assigned to tasks that they believe they are capable of performing. An employee needs to perceive that the work environment is conducive to success.

2. The organization must make rewards contingent on good performance. Employees should know that performing well leads to being rewarded.

3. The organization must choose rewards that employees want. Individuals must be able to acquire the things or experience the outcomes that have valence for them.

Equity theory:
A second endogenous theory of motivation is equity theory. Equity theory explores the effects that social comparison between employees will have on individuals' performance. Equity theory explains that not only does the actual value of rewards matter, but so does the relative value when compared to the rewards received by co-workers. More specifically, equity theory suggests that individuals create a ratio of their inputs (effort, time, abilities) to their outcomes (pay, recognition, benefits) in order to determine the fairness of their rewards. Equity theory can be summarized by two equations: **Equity occurs when**

$$I_s / O_s = I_0 / O_0$$

where I_s is the inputs for self

O_S are the outcomes for self

I_O is the inputs for the comparison individual (other)

O_O are the outcomes for the other person.

In contrast, **inequity occurs when**
$$I_S / O_S > I_O / O_O \quad \text{or} \quad I_S / O_S < I_O / O_O$$

If these ratios are the same, there is perceived equity and the employee is not motivated to change the inputs or outcomes in the situation. If these ratios are different, then the employee is motivated to restore equity. Inequity is perceived when individuals believe that they are under-rewarded relative to the other and when they perceive that they are over-rewarded relative to the other.

Equity theory suggests that individuals may take a variety of actions in order to restore equity.

1. They may objectively change the outcomes or inputs for themselves.
2. They may objectively change the outcomes or inputs for the comparison individual.
3. They may psychologically change the inputs or outcomes for themselves.
4. They may psychologically change the inputs or outcomes for the comparison individual.
5. They may select a different comparison individual.
6. They may withdraw from the situation.

The action chosen to restore equity will depend on the degree of perceived inequity, the constraints on the individual, and the individual's perception about which action is most likely to restore equity (Adams, 1963). For example, a police officer might create her input to outcomes ratio by analyzing the hours that she puts in, the years she spent in school and training, her four years of experience on the job, and her perceived level of ability. She evaluates those inputs against the high risk in her job, her salary, the recognition she receives from the supervisor, and the relationships that she has with her co-workers on the police force. Having established this ratio, she may identify her partner as a relevant individual for comparison. She will attempt to assess his inputs: the hours that he puts in, his education, training and experience, and her perceptions of his ability. She will also attempt to estimate his outcomes: she may know what his salary is, she observes the recognition that he gets from the supervisor, understands the risk of his job, and observes his relationships with others on the police force.

If she believes that her input to outcomes ratio is different from his, she will be motivated to establish equity. If the police officer finds that her partner has similar training and education, assumes that he has similar abilities and puts in similar hours, but finds that he is paid more, and notices that he receives more attention from the supervisor, she may take one of many possible actions. She may ask her supervisor for a raise and discuss her need for feedback (objectively increasing her outcomes). She could psychologically alter the outcomes by reinterpreting them and deciding that she has better relationships with her co-workers that are very meaningful to her. She may reduce her input by working fewer hours or reducing her level of effort, or she may quit to look for another job in which she believes she will be treated equitably.

Equity theory suggests that individuals will be motivated to restore equity when the ratios are unequal regardless of whether the discrepancy benefits the individual or not. In other words, it suggests that our police officer would also initiate change if she believes that she is overpaid in comparison to her partner (or if her partner is the one to discover the inequity, he will attempt to restore equity). Research on equity theory has consistently shown support for the theory under conditions of underpayment. Individuals typically reduce their inputs in the form of quality or quantity of work. In contrast, the research is less conclusive under conditions of overpayment. Individuals do not consistently increase their quantity or quality of performance to compensate for the higher level of outcomes that they are receiving (Campbell & Pritchard, 1976).

Greenberg (1990) used equity theory to explain how employees might respond to a sudden pay cut. Greenberg studied three manufacturing plants belonging to the same company which produced mechanical parts for aerospace and automotive industries. The study lasted for 30 weeks during which Greenberg observed the theft rates and voluntary employee turnover (the number of people who quit their jobs). During the first ten weeks of the study (before the pay cut) and the last ten weeks of the study (after pay had been restored) the wages paid at the three plants were essentially equivalent. During weeks 11 through 20, the loss of a large contract required a 15 percent pay cut for the employees at two of the plants (A and B).

In addition, the announcements of the pay cut were handled differently at these two plants. At plant A, the pay cut was announced by the company president and was thoroughly explained during a one hour meeting with all employees. Workers were told that the pay cut was necessary to avoid layoffs, that all employees would share in the pay cut, and that it would be temporary. Employees at plant A were given time to ask questions and were repeatedly told that the company regretted having to take this action. In contrast, the pay cut was briefly described (in a 15 minute meeting) by a company vice-president at plant B. Employees were told that a loss of contract made the cut necessary, but were given no additional information and the vice-president did not express the company's regret. Plant C received no pay cut.

During the 10 weeks of the pay cut the theft and turnover rates at the three plants were significantly different. At plant C, where no pay cut had occurred, the theft rate and voluntary turnover rate was consistent throughout the 30 week period. The theft rate was approximately 3% of the total inventory and approximately 5% of the workforce left the company voluntarily during this time. At plant A, in which the employees received a thorough explanation of the pay cut, the theft rate was slightly higher during the pay cut than during the first and last ten weeks of the study (approximately 6% of the total inventory). The turnover rate at plant A was stable throughout the 30-week period.

At plant B, in which the employees received a brief and inadequate explanation of the pay cut, the theft rate and voluntary turnover rates were substantially higher during weeks 11 through 20. The theft rate rose to nearly 9% of total inventory and the turnover rate was approximately 23% during this time. These employees also reported the greatest perceptions of inequity. Figure 4 shows the comparisons between these three plants during the 30 week study. Greenberg (1990) suggests that these differences in theft and turnover rates represent attempts by the employees to restore equity between their inputs and outcomes during a pay cut. Because their outcomes had been reduced by the pay cut, the employees at plants A and B increased these outcomes by stealing from the employer. In addition, this research implies that employers can influence perceptions of equity by thoroughly explaining the ways in which rewards are being distributed. Showing sincere concern for employees and providing thorough explanations seems to reduce the perceptions of inequity and inhibit the actions that might be taken to restore it.

In a second study, researchers attempted to integrate the predictions of equity and expectancy theories. In a study of Major League Baseball free agents, Harder (1991) attempted to

98

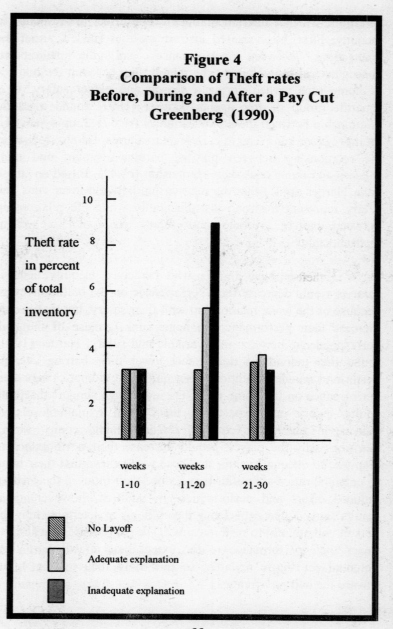

Figure 4
Comparison of Theft rates
Before, During and After a Pay Cut
Greenberg (1990)

Theft rate in percent of total inventory

weeks 1-10   weeks 11-20   weeks 21-30

No Layoff

Adequate explanation

Inadequate explanation

determine whether instrumentalities would affect the response to inequity. First, he measured instrumentalities (beliefs about the connections between performance and the anticipated consequences) by looking at the relationship between the number of home runs earned during a season and player salary, in a separate group of free agents. Harder (1991) found a strong relationship between these two variables ($r=.57$). Employees who hit more home runs tend to earn higher salaries. He also looked at the relationship between players' batting averages and their salaries and found a weaker relationship ($r=.42$). Based on these data, Harder argues that the relationship between home runs and salary represent a strong instrumentality while the relationship between batting average and salary represents a weaker instrumentality.

He hypothesized that players who perceived inequity in their salaries would decrease their performance on the batting average because of the weak relationship with their salary, but they would increase their performance on home runs because of the high correspondence between that variable and salary. Harder (1991) found that individuals did in fact lower their batting average performance under conditions of inequity, but did not change their performance on the home runs. These findings suggest that both equity theory and expectancy theory can explain levels of motivation and observed performance. First, equity theory describes why the players would decrease their performance in response to unequal treatment. Those who believe that their input to outcome ratios are unfair may reduce their input in the form of reduced effort and performance. In addition, however, these results suggest that expectancy theory helps to determine how the person will attempt to restore equity. The players are unwilling to lower their performance to the extent that it will hurt their potential for future rewards, so they only reduce their inputs toward the batting average.

Both of these studies represent strong efforts to study motivation in actual work environments. Much of the earlier work on these theories was conducted short term in laboratory settings. Both Greenberg's (1990) and Harder's (1991) work suggest that these theories can explain behavior of employees and provide support for motivational programs which take these factors into account.

Motivational Practices: Programs Used to Improve Performance

In addition to developing theories and models to explain and predict the motivation and performance level of employees, industrial and organizational psychologists have used this understanding to create programs that can be implemented to improve the productivity of individuals and organizations. These interventions focus on how employers can facilitate the effective work performance of their employees.

Goal Setting and Management By Objectives

Many organizations have turned to goal setting programs and the more complex Management By Objectives (MBO) to enhance the performance of their employees. Goal setting programs have been developed from the research on goal theory. These programs have been applied to a variety of jobs including sales, management, engineering, and clerical jobs, and have reported up to 10 to 25% improvements in performance (Pritchard, Roth, Jones, Galgay & Watson, 1986). In effective goal setting programs, employees or supervisors set goals based on clear organizational objectives. These goals help individual employees identify their roles within the organization and its mission. Goals also provide employees with information about what needs to be done in order to reach those organizational objectives. Goal setting can be applied in two ways. If goals are established as minimum standards of performance, they will generally have little motivational value, but employees who do not reach their goals can be reprimanded. In contrast, when goals are set as high standards to be strived for they have a strong motivational effect. Goal attainment is rewarded and can be publicized, allowing for the additional benefits of recognition as a reward (Pritchard et al., 1986).

One outgrowth of goal setting as a motivational program has been the development of **management by objectives (MBO)**. MBO combines goal setting, participative decision making, and regular, objective feedback into a comprehensive motivational system. The first step in MBO is to set organizational objectives and determine how attainment of those objectives will be measured (a step that is also critical for successful selection and training). Next both employees and their supervisors propose personal work goals and suggest how performance on those goals should be measured. Third, the employees and their supervisors come to an agreement about the goals and measures. Fourth, the employees receive feedback about their progress toward the goals. At this point, inappropriate goals may be discarded or revised. Finally, both the individual's goal attainment and organizational performance are evaluated and the process repeats itself.

MBO may enhance performance because employees have a clear understanding of what is expected of them and know how their performance will be evaluated. Also, employees have some control over their work goals. In addition, MBO encourages frequent communication between employees and their supervisors both when setting goals and receiving feedback about performance. Management by objectives has been shown to be most effective in enhancing organizational productivity when there is thorough support from upper-level management and when all individuals within the organization use this program. MBO may be less effective when there is limited commitment from top management and the practice is only applied at the middle and lower levels of the organization (Rodgers & Hunter, 1991).

Incentive Programs

Many workers report that there is little connection between their work performance and the financial rewards that they receive (Lawler, 1987). To change this, some organizations have used the principles of reinforcement theory to design more effective financial incentive programs and to facilitate improved performance among their employees. Pay can be an effective motivator for individual employees when it is important to them and when it is tied to their performance in obvious ways. While you might expect that money is one of the primary motivators for good work performance, it is frequently not used in ways that will facilitate improved performance. Unfortunately, the traditional hourly wage or annual salary is only weakly connected to daily performance and is a weak motivator. Except at the extremes, employees can improve or reduce their performance levels without any change in their immediate financial rewards. Pay increases are frequently only awarded on a semi-annual or annual basis. In contrast, incentive systems in which performance is closely tied to pay, are frequently effective motivators. Employees may be paid on a piece rate system in which the employee is paid for each item produced or sold, raises may be awarded on the basis of reaching performance goals, or bonuses may be awarded to individuals who achieve high levels of performance. By making financial rewards more closely related to job performance, employees are more likely to maintain good performance.

Although incentives given to individual employees should encourage the optimal level of performance from each employee, many organizations have implemented group incentive plans because they are more easily administered and they encourage cooperation within work groups. Group incentive plans are based on the attainment of group goals or objectives. Groups of workers are paid on the basis of their performance as a unit such as a team, division, or plant. Though pay may be less contingent on the performance of any given employee, these incentive plans can effectively facilitate cooperation among workers and encourage peer pressure to improve productivity. To demonstrate the positive outcomes associated with group incentive plans, Petty, Singleton and Connell (1992) compared the performance of two divisions of a utility company. They found that the division under the group incentive plan showed reduced costs of operation, improved productivity, and more positive attitudes when compared to a division in the same company which did not have this incentive program. The plan used in this study included group financial incentives, regular and specific feedback to individual employees and work groups, and employee participation and involvement to enhance performance.

Knowledge-Based Pay

A third motivational program focuses on developing employees' skills and creating a flexible, knowledgeable, and well-trained workforce. In **knowledge-based pay**, employees are paid on the basis of the skills that they have mastered, not seniority or units of production. This system encourages employees to expand their work-related knowledge. Typically, in order to be paid for having a particular skill, employees must demonstrate mastery or proficiency after receiving training and may be required to be recertified at regular intervals to ensure that the skills are being maintained. Knowledge-based pay may be used in conjunction with team work. Employees are given a pay increase when they have mastered all the jobs performed by the team. Once team members can perform all of these jobs, then they can rotate through them, facilitating job variety and team flexibility. Knowledge-based pay systems can also have some drawbacks for both the employees and employers. First, training costs are high for the organization because more people are typically trained to perform a certain set of tasks and the training must be frequently available for the employees who want or need to learn those tasks. Second, if training occurs during work hours, the company is not

104

immediately benefiting from the employees' efforts. If training is offered after regular work hours, the employees may resent having to use their own time to learn the new jobs. Finally, some employees may resent the pressure from the company or the team members to keep learning new jobs.

Section Summary

The study of workplace motivation emphasizes understanding the factors which direct employees efforts toward certain tasks, determine the level of effort put toward those tasks, and maintain that effort over time. Overall, when studying motivation in the workplace and developing motivational programs I/O psychologists are attempting to enhance the productivity of individuals and organizations. A variety of theories have been developed to explain work motivation. These theories fall into two main categories. Exogenous theories of motivation emphasize the factors that can be manipulated by the employer to change the employees' behavior. This category includes need theories such as Maslow's need hierarchy and McClelland's need for achievement, goal theory, and reinforcement theory. The second category of motivational theories is endogenous, which focus on how individual interpretations of the work and work environment affect motivation. This category includes expectancy theory and equity theory.

Research on work motivation reveals a complex process and many of these theories can explain at least some observed work behavior. These motivational theories have led to the development of many motivational programs designed to improve productivity within organizations. Goal setting and Management by Objectives developed out of goal theory and various incentive systems show the influence of reinforcement theory.

Job Satisfaction: The Meaning of Work

The study of motivation and the practices that have developed from this research are designed to enhance the effectiveness of the employee. Although the individual employee may benefit from this increased productivity, the focus has been on the positive outcomes for the employer which is better able to reach organizational objectives. In this next section you will read about how I/O psychologists study and design programs to modify employee attitudes about their work. The primary focus of this work is to enhance the positive reactions that employees have toward their work and work environment.

Why are Job Attitudes Important?

Why are some employees satisfied with their work while others are not? How does work fit into other aspects of a person's life? These questions suggest a second set of work outcomes that are important in I/O psychology: work attitudes. While the emphasis of research and interventions of motivation has been to enhance the productivity of the individual employees and therefore benefit primarily the organization, the focus of research and interventions of job satisfaction has been to enhance the benefits that the employee receives from the work.

Job satisfaction can be generally defined as the positive or negative evaluations that an employee makes of his or her work environment (O'Reilly, 1991). Industrial/organizational psychologists have looked at job satisfaction from two angles. One area of research and practice has focused on identifying the sources of job satisfaction, understanding why some employees are more satisfied than others. Early work in this field focused on determining if specific subgroups of employees differed in their levels of job satisfaction. For example are older employees more satisfied than younger employees? Are women less satisfied than men at work? Are employees at higher levels of the organization more satisfied than employees at the lower levels of the organization? More recently, research on job satisfaction has focused on job characteristics such as the degree of independence an employee has, the amount of variety found in the tasks he or she is asked to perform, or the relationships with co-workers and supervisors.

The second area of research and practice in job satisfaction has emphasized understanding the consequences of job satisfaction. How do employees behave when they are satisfied and how do they react when they are dissatisfied with their work. I/O psychologists working on these questions have investigated negative consequences such as turnover and absenteeism, arguing that dissatisfied employees may be more likely to withdraw from the work environment than their satisfied colleagues. Researchers attempting to understand the consequences of satisfaction have also searched for a relationship between satisfaction and productivity. Is it possible to satisfy the individual employees while simultaneously reaching the organization's objectives? Interventions have been designed to improve work-related attitudes with the hope of reducing the likelihood of withdrawal or increasing productivity.

Theories About the Sources of Job Satisfaction

Facet Models of Job Satisfaction
A friend tells you that he hates his job. One of the first questions you are likely to consider is "what doesn't he like about it?" Facet models of job satisfaction suggest that employees are typically dissatisfied with specific features or facets of their work such as uncomfortable working conditions, unfriendly or incompetent co-workers, long or irregular hours, or boring, monotonous tasks. Facet models of job satisfaction have developed out of various attempts to measure job satisfaction and to identify the sources of

satisfaction or dissatisfaction within the work environment. These models describe overall job satisfaction as a composite which reflects the degree of satisfaction with **job facets**: distinct features of the job such as pay, co-workers, supervision, and recognition.

In one facet model, Lawler (1973) describes job satisfaction as the difference between what individuals perceive they should receive from the job and what they actually receive from their jobs. He argues that if individuals receive less than they think they should, then they will feel dissatisfied. If they receive what they believe they should be receiving, then they will be satisfied, and if they receive more than they think that they should receive, they will feel guilty and uncomfortable. This comparison is based on the individual's evaluation of separate components of the work to create overall satisfaction with the job. For example, a physician's overall job satisfaction reflects her satisfaction with the various features of the work such as the work schedule, the challenge and variety in the work, and the sense of accomplishment. This satisfaction is a function of what the doctor believes she should experience from her work and what she actually gets from it.

Similarly, Locke (1976) suggested that job satisfaction could be broken down into evaluations of different aspects of the work and work environment. Overall job satisfaction is an unweighted summary of those evaluations. To understand this summary, we must first know the importance of each facet to the individual employee. If a particular facet of the job, such as pay, is very important to the employee, then the range of reaction is wide. The employee can feel very positive or very negative about his or her pay. In contrast, if a facet such as job status is not particularly important to the employee, then the range of reaction will be fairly limited. The employee will not have a strong reaction (either positive or negative) to his or her job status because it is not important. Locke argues that the importance of a facet to the individual determines its contribution to overall satisfaction by determining this range of reaction. The more important facets contribute more to the overall composite because the employee has a stronger reaction to them. Rice, Gentile and McFarlin (1991), found evidence to support Locke's theory. In a study of employed college students, these researchers found that when a facet was important to the employee there was a wider range of affective reaction than when the facet was of little importance to the individual.

Herzberg's Two Factor Theory

In a second theory of job satisfaction, Herzberg (1968) suggests that different facets of work and work environments affect the level of job satisfaction and dissatisfaction in particular ways. More specifically, Herzberg (1968) suggested that satisfaction and dissatisfaction with work were not opposites on the same continuum. Instead, Herzberg found that there were elements of work activities and the work environment that would influence satisfaction with work and that there were different facets of work that would affect an employee's dissatisfaction.

Herzberg proposed a two factor theory in which there are **hygiene factors** which could influence the level of dissatisfaction and **motivating factors** which could influence the level of satisfaction. Herzberg described hygiene factors to include physical and psychological elements of the work environment such as pleasant or competent co-workers, effective relationships with the supervisor, good working conditions (low-risk, safe, or noise free) and appropriate work schedules. When these factors are not present, the employee will be dissatisfied. When these factors are present the employee is no longer dissatisfied but is neutral. In other words, the hygiene factors will only affect the level of dissatisfaction and cannot make an individual satisfied with his or her work. In contrast, the motivating factors are aspects of the work itself such as a high level of challenge or the degree to which the individual employee has a strong sense of accomplishment and achievement from the work done. When present, these factors will make the individual satisfied with his or her work. When these factors are absent, the individual has a neutral attitude but is not dissatisfied. The presence of motivating factors only influences the level of satisfaction that the employee experiences, not the degree of dissatisfaction. For example, a computer programmer may be satisfied with his job because he enjoys the work itself and receives frequent recognition from his supervisor for the good work that he does. According to Herzberg, if the computer programmer does not receive this recognition and does not really enjoy the work, he will not be satisfied, but he will not be dissatisfied either. In contrast, the computer programmer may be dissatisfied with his working conditions and dislikes many of his co-workers. If the organization improves his working conditions and he moves into a new work group and likes his new co-workers, he will no longer be dissatisfied, but will not be satisfied with his job because of these changes.

While Herzberg's theory has been widely accepted by managers and has much intuitive appeal, the empirical support for the theory is less impressive. In support of the theory, Herzberg studied over 600 workers in a variety of job categories including hospital maintenance, nursing, military, teaching, accounting and management. Employees were asked to describe the events which led to extreme dissatisfaction and extreme satisfaction with their work. He found that 81% of the factors leading to satisfaction could be identified as motivating factors. Sixty-nine percent of the factors leading to dissatisfaction were labeled as hygiene factors (Herzberg, 1968).

In a second study comparing the work values and satisfaction of managers and skilled workers, Lahiri and Srivastva (1967) found evidence to support Herzberg's contention that satisfaction and dissatisfaction represent different constructs, but they did not find evidence to support his division of hygiene and motivating factors.

The intrinsic elements of the work (opportunities for growth, achievement or recognition) were more likely to affect satisfaction and the extrinsic elements of the work (pay, co-workers, or working conditions) were more likely to affect dissatisfaction, but the results did not suggest the clean division that Herzberg proposes.

Job Characteristics Model

I/O psychologists have suggested that there are specific ways in which the various aspects of the job environment identified by Herzberg (1968), Locke (1976) and Lawler (1973) influence individuals' job attitudes. Specifically, Hackman and Oldham (1976) proposed a comprehensive model that describes how job characteristics such as the variety of tasks that employees perform or the degree of responsibility that an individual has affect the meaning that work has. This model, labeled the **job characteristics model** speculates that all jobs can be described on five basic dimensions:

1. **Skill variety**: the variety of skills, tasks and abilities needed to perform the job. Some jobs such as an office manager require many different skills, while others such as a data entry clerk are more repetitive and monotonous.
2. **Task identity**: the degree to which the individual can experience the completion of a process or see a finished product. Jobs such as that of a graphic artist require work on a project from the early, idea stage through the completed project, while others such as assembly line work may only experience a small portion of the work process.
3. **Task significance**: the degree to which the job is seen as important to others. Jobs such as nursing are viewed as very important to the patients and doctors, while other jobs such as that of an archivist are seen as less critical.
4. **Autonomy**: the degree to which an individual employee can determine how to do the work or when to do it. Jobs such as that of a college professor have a high degree of independence

or autonomy, while others such as a receptionist are given firm guidelines and have little choice about when and how to do the work.

5. **Task feedback**: it reflects the extent to which an individual can receive clear information about the effectiveness of his or her performance of the tasks that are required. Salespeople generally receive clear and regular feedback, while others such as artists may receive more ambiguous information about the quality of their work.

Hackman and Oldham (1976) suggest that the extent to which a job has these features determines the effect that the job has on the individual's work attitudes and work outcomes. Jobs that are high on these dimensions should result in high degrees of motivation, high quality work performance, high levels of satisfaction, and low levels of turnover and absenteeism. The researchers also point out that jobs with these characteristics will not affect all employees in the same way. Individuals who have high levels of **growth need strength**, a need to seek higher order growth and achievement needs, will benefit from jobs with these characteristics more so than employees with lower levels of those needs.

The research on the job characteristics model is at least partially supportive. Employees in jobs that have these characteristics do report higher levels of motivation and job satisfaction. Spector and Jex (1991) found a significant correlation between the reported job characteristics and reported job satisfaction. There is a relationship between how employees view their jobs and how they evaluate them. These evaluations are then related to the intent to quit the job with individuals who are more satisfied being less likely to indicate that they intend to leave the job. Unfortunately there is less evidence to suggest that these kinds of jobs consistently facilitate higher levels of performance or lower levels of turnover and absenteeism (Spector and Jex, 1991).

113

How do these job characteristics lead to higher levels of motivation and higher levels of satisfaction in employees? James and Tetrick (1986) suggest that job satisfaction reflects an individual's cognitive interpretations of his or her work environment. Their research indicates that the evaluations of that environment (overall job satisfaction) also influence the way in which the individual interprets and views the job environment. In other words, the employee's view of his or her work environment influences his or her overall job satisfaction. In addition, overall job satisfaction influences how the employee interprets work events. More specifically, if an international marketing manager believes that she has significant responsibilities, opportunities for advancement and growth and is well compensated, she may experience high overall job satisfaction. In addition, that high level of satisfaction may cause her to overlook her low level of job security or the lack of support that she receives from her supervisor.

James and James (1989) propose that the relationship between job characteristics and overall job satisfaction reflects self-interest. Individual employees may interpret their work environments by assessing the degree to which the job and its features are beneficial or harmful to them. The belief that the job and its elements are beneficial is more likely to result in overall satisfaction and while the belief that its components may be harmful will probably lead to overall dissatisfaction. For example, if a high school counselor believes that his work provides him with a sense of accomplishment, the hours allow him to spend time with his family and pursue his hobbies, and his salary is adequate to meet his primary needs, then he is likely to be satisfied. In contrast, if this counselor believes that he is unable to effect much change in his clients and feels his pay is not sufficient to meet his needs, he will be dissatisfied.

114

While the research results described above suggest that job characteristics influence overall satisfaction, and that overall satisfaction then may influence an employee's intention to quit, others have proposed a different relationship. Doran, Stone, Brief, and George (1991) have suggested that the primary direction of the relationship should focus on the intentions to quit and their effects on the individual's evaluation and interpretation of the work environment. Doran et al., (1991) argue that the intent to leave a job can predict the individual's level of job satisfaction. In other words, people who intend to quit their jobs will develop a lower level of satisfaction. These researchers also found that this relationship between intent and satisfaction is moderated by the individual's degree of economic requirements. Individuals who had low economic requirements (those who did not need the financial benefits of the work) were likely to report lower levels of job satisfaction if they intend to quit and higher job satisfaction if they did not. In contrast, among those who were more dependent on the financial rewards from the work there was not a relationship between their intent to leave and their job satisfaction.

Job Satisfaction as a Disposition

Recent work in job satisfaction has explored a different source of the variation between individual employees. Some researchers have shown that job satisfaction is relatively stable across time and jobs for individuals (Arvey, Bouchard, Segal, & Abraham, 1989; Keller, Bouchard, Arvey, Segal and Dawis, 1992; Bouchard, Arvey, Keller, & Segal, 1992; Shaffer, 1987; Staw, 1991; Staw & Ross, 1985). Staw and his colleagues have re-analyzed a series of longitudinal studies and found convincing evidence for consistency in job attitudes such as job satisfaction across time. Staw and Ross (1985) found that individuals' job satisfaction was relatively stable over three to five year periods even when they changed jobs or when they changed both jobs and occupations. This finding suggests that despite changes in supervisors, work environments and conditions, co-workers, and work procedures, individuals maintain similar levels of job satisfaction. Changes in the job characteristics do not lead to significant changes in the levels of job satisfaction. In a second study, Staw (1991) reports that measures of affective disposition (positive and negative evaluations of life events and circumstances) taken during adolescence predicted job and career satisfaction measured more than 40 years later during middle and late career stages. He argues that one of the reasons that efforts to increase the satisfaction of workers have been disappointing is because these dispositional features of job satisfaction make these attitudes more resistant to change. One potential explanation is that employees who report high levels of job satisfaction at one time, and on one job, are also likely to be satisfied later regardless of job changes that may have occurred (Hulin, 1991).

In contrast, a competing hypothesis for these observed relationships would be that people choose jobs with similar characteristics even when they change jobs. Well-educated or highly skilled people tend to have jobs with desirable characteristics. Similarly, less well-trained individuals with less education and fewer skills are likely to have more routine work with lower pay and poorer working conditions. These individuals will continue to report lower levels of job satisfaction following job change. These views summarize the competing explanations for the stability in job satisfaction. Individuals are likely to keep similar jobs over time and we therefore might expect consistency in attitudes. However, this consistency could also be a personality or dispositional factor.

Other researchers have taken these observations one step further and suggested that there is evidence to support the heritability of job attitudes such as satisfaction (Arvey, et al., 1989; Keller et al., 1992; Bouchard et al., 1992; Shaffer, 1987). You may remember the discussion of the heritability index from your study of individual differences and psychological testing. A heritability index represents the proportion of variation among individuals on a particular characteristic that is attributed to genetic variation. In a study of 34 pairs of identical twins reared apart, Arvey et al., (1989) found that roughly 30% of the variation in job satisfaction among the participants in the study could be attributed to genetics and that many of the twins held similar jobs. In a similar study of identical twins, fraternal twins and their spouses, Keller et al., (1992) found a heritability index of .4 for work related values such as achievement, comfort, status, safety, and autonomy and suggest that there may a predisposition for individuals to prefer some outcomes over others. This index means that 40% of the variation among individuals in this study is attributed to genetic differences and 60% is attributed to environmental differences. These researchers suggest that the genetic influence on these preferences is indirect. Individuals are probably not born with a set of work-related preferences but instead genetics affect the way in which children develop preferences for things and outcomes (Keller et al., 1992). Similarly, Shaffer (1987) presents evidence of dispositional influences on job attitudes by showing the relationship between work and non-work attitudes over time.

While the research reveals a certain amount of stability in work attitudes such as job satisfaction, these researchers do not argue that job satisfaction and other job attitudes cannot be changed by modifying elements of the work or work environment (Keller et al., 1992; Bouchard et al., 1992; Staw, 1991). In contrast, most I/O psychologists indicate that despite this apparent stability, the job environment is a very important source of job satisfaction. Organizations can modify job satisfaction by improving the characteristics of the work and work environment, but there may be boundaries for the amount of change in attitudes that can be expected for individuals. For example, these results imply that organizations should first understand the preferences of different individuals, and then modify the work and work environment in order to maximize that individual's satisfaction. Fortunately I/O psychologists may not really need to thoroughly understand the source of this stability in order to design effective interventions. Instead, they must recognize that there is stability and will counteract the efforts to change satisfaction through changes in the work environment made by the organization (Hulin, 1991).

Consequences of Job Satisfaction and Dissatisfaction

In addition to determining the sources or antecedents of job satisfaction, researchers have attempted to find the connections between an employee's level of job satisfaction or dissatisfaction and the behaviors that he or she exhibits at work. First, what are the consequences of job dissatisfaction for the organization? Are dissatisfied employees more likely to leave the organization or to miss work? Are dissatisfied employees likely to be less productive than satisfied employees? Are dissatisfied individuals more likely to harm the organization in some way? Second, what are the consequences of dissatisfaction for the individual employees? What is the relationship to levels of life satisfaction and what are the implications for their psychological well-being?

Organizational Withdrawal
One prominent concern about the consequences of dissatisfaction has focused on organizational withdrawal. Organizational withdrawal is a broad term that encompasses a variety of behaviors which remove the employee physically or psychologically from the work environment. At one extreme, the employee may leave the organization; this process is labeled as **turnover**. Other employees may be absent from or late for work; these behaviors are labeled **absenteeism** and **tardiness**. Finally some employees may be less focused on the work that has to be done and less active in the workplace by taking frequent breaks, spending more time discussing non-work activities with other employees or daydreaming (Hulin, 1991). Although results from

118

the particular studies differ, overall job satisfaction generally has a strong negative relationship with turnover, a moderate negative relationship with absenteeism, and a weak negative relationship with tardiness (Hulin, 1991).

One popular model of employee withdrawal focuses on the steps which precede voluntary turnover (Mobley, 1977; Mobley, Horner, & Hollingsworth, 1978). How does an employee reach the decision to quit his or her job? This model of the turnover process involves nine steps beginning with the evaluation of the existing job (which leads to the level of experienced job satisfaction and dissatisfaction) and ending with the decision to quit or stay with the organization. Table 4 outlines these steps in greater detail. In between, the individual will think about quitting, determine the pros and cons of quitting, search for job alternatives, evaluate those alternatives, and develop an intention to quit or stay in the job.

In a recent test of Mobley's model, Gerhart (1991) found support for many of the steps between dissatisfaction and turnover. Gerhart (1990) surveyed approximately 1400 young employees who were working at least 15 hours per week. First, Gerhart found that perceived ease of movement to other jobs was positively related to regional unemployment levels. Individuals believe that it will be harder to get another job when the unemployment rates are high and easier to get another job when those rates are low. Second, the intention to stay with an organization was negatively related to the perceived ease of movement and positively related to job satisfaction. Employees who believe they can get another job are more likely to think about leaving the organization, and individuals with high levels of

Table 4
Steps in Mobley's Process Model
of Organizational Turnover

1. Evaluate existing job.

2. Experience job satisfaction/dissatisfaction.

3. Consider quitting.

4. Evaluate potential usefulness of job search and costs of quitting.

5. Intention to search for alternative jobs.

6. Active search for alternative jobs.

7. Evaluate job alternatives.

8. Compare alternatives to present job.

9. Intention to quit or stay.

10. Decision to quit or stay.

satisfaction are less likely to think about leaving the current job. Finally, Gerhart found an interaction between perceived ease of movement and the intention to stay with the organization. Job dissatisfaction leads to intentions to leave when individuals believe that they can readily find other work. While Mobley's (1977) model of turnover has received much attention and considerable support, there are concerns about its lack of specificity at certain steps in the process. For example, when the individual evaluates the present job in comparison to the existing alternatives how does that information affect the individual's perceived level of satisfaction or dissatisfaction?

Because of financial and other obligations, quitting may not always be an option for an employee. Instead of leaving the organization, employees may select alternative withdrawal behaviors that will also remove them from the dissatisfying situation such as being absent, late, or inattentive to work demands. I/O psychologists have attempted to understand how employees choose between these withdrawal behaviors. One potential explanation is called a **compensatory model.** According to this view, individuals will select from a set of withdrawal behaviors in order to reduce the tension caused by being in a dissatisfying environment. A dissatisfied employee experiences a constant amount of tension caused by being in a dissatisfying environment. Individuals will choose from a set of withdrawal behaviors in a way to reduce that tension. They may choose many minor withdrawal behaviors or one that is more severe. For example, an employee may choose to be absent some of the time and to spend less time working when he or she is at work, while another employee may choose to be late and absent some of the time (Hulin, 1991).

In contrast, the **progression of withdrawal model** proposes that individuals gradually exhibit more extreme withdrawal behaviors if the first choices are not successful in relieving the tension. For example, an engineer may daydream or take long lunch breaks when he first begins to experience job dissatisfaction. If these behaviors are not effective, he may begin arriving late for work and leaving early. If these withdrawal behaviors are not effective he may begin missing work.

Up to this point we have been discussing turnover as voluntary, the employee decides to terminate his or her relationship with the organization. Recent research suggests that organizations must also be concerned about the effects of layoffs on productivity, and organizational outcomes. Layoffs not only hurt the individuals who lose the job, but can have severe consequences for the individuals who stay with the organization (Brockner, 1990). Brockner conducted two studies to investigate the effects of involuntary turnover on the attitudes and performance of the survivors. First, in a field study, Brockner surveyed nearly 600 retail employees. Participants reported the degree to which they had close working or personal relationships with recently laid-off employees, the degree to which they felt that the layoffs had been adequately explained, the degree to which the survivors felt that the layoff victims had been taken care of, and their reported change in commitment to the company. In this study, Brockner (1990) found that layoff survivors who knew the victims of the layoff and felt that the organization had used unfair layoff practices reported greater decreases in their commitment to the company. In other words, employees who knew layoff victims and felt that these people had been treated unfairly, reported that they now had lower levels of commitment to the company.

While the evidence from this study is compelling, there are some flaws in this research method. Research results depended on retrospective reports from the layoff survivors. The employees were asked to describe their relationships with the layoff victims, their understanding of the layoff process, and their changes in commitment; these memories may include distortions of the actual events and experiences. In addition, because of the industry that was studied, most of the participants were female; there may be gender differences in these perceptions.

To overcome these flaws, Brockner designed a second study to observe the performance of participants after they had been exposed to either a fair, unfair, or no layoff manipulation in a laboratory experiment. Participants were told that they would be doing a proofreading task and would eventually be working with a second individual (who was actually a confederate working for the experimenter). The participants first completed an attitude survey and were given false feedback on the results. Half of the participants were led to believe that the confederate had similar political, social, and economic attitudes (labeled the high inclusion condition) while the other half of the participants were led to believe that the confederate had different attitudes (labeled the low inclusion condition). Participants were then exposed to one of three layoff conditions: a low caretaking condition in which the confederate was told that he or she was no longer needed and could not be paid for his or her time (this person protested mildly), a high caretaking layoff condition in which the confederate was told that he or she was no longer needed but would be paid for his or her participation to this point (this person indicated that this seemed fair), and a no layoff condition.

Brockner found a significant interaction between the degree of perceived similarity of the confederate and the layoff condition. Participants who thought the confederate was similar performed at a lower level in the low caretaking condition than in either the high caretaking or no layoff condition. In contrast, individuals who thought the confederate was different from themselves performed at similar levels for the various caretaking conditions. Figure 5 outlines the results from this study. Brockner (1990) suggests that the results of these studies combined indicate that layoffs will have the most negative effects on the attitudes and

123

Figure 5
Summary of results from Brockner (1990)

Attitude Similarity

Layoff Condition	High Inclusion	Low Inclusion
High Caretaking	No change in performance after layoff occurred	No change in performance after layoff occurred
Low Caretaking	Reduced performance after the layoff occurred	No change in performance after layoff occurred
No Layoff	No change in performance	No change in performance

performance of the remaining employees when they were familiar and friendly with the layoff victims and believe that those individuals have been treated unfairly.

Productivity

While the expected relationship between job satisfaction and organizational withdrawal has been largely supported, the relationship between levels of job satisfaction and effective performance or productivity is much more tenuous. Happy employees are not necessarily productive employees. Though initially surprising, there are a number of factors which can explain this relationship. First, while performance depends in part on the abilities of the worker, the degree of satisfaction largely does not. Second, there is evidence to suggest that some individuals consistently put more effort into their work than others. In other words, people who work hard in one context are likely to work hard in other contexts (Staw, 1991). Finally, there is some evidence that while satisfaction does not necessarily enhance productivity, good performance of the job may enhance the employee's satisfaction with the job (Porter and Lawler, 1968).

Life Satisfaction and Psychological Well-Being

Does the degree of job satisfaction affect an individual's psychological well-being or degree of overall life satisfaction? Winefield, Winefield, Tiggemann and Goldney (1991) found evidence that job satisfaction has a number of positive consequences for individuals. These researchers studied a group of over 400 individuals while they were in school and again eight years later. They classified individuals into four categories according to their current status: satisfied employed, full-time students, dissatisfied employed, and unemployed. Individuals in the satisfied employed and student groups had higher levels of self-esteem, and were less likely to feel depressed than those in the unemployed and dissatisfied employed groups. Similarly, the satisfied employed individuals reported less frequent negative moods than individuals in all other groups. One of the most interesting aspects of these findings is that the differences found between the groups after eight years were due primarily to improvements for the satisfied employed individuals and students rather than in a deterioration for the dissatisfied employed and unemployed individuals. These results would seem to suggest that for younger workers, working at a satisfying job or being a full time student enhances psychological well-being but that dissatisfying work or unemployment does not necessarily have detrimental effects. The authors are quick to point out, however, that these finding may not transfer to older employees. Other research suggests that the consequences of unemployment can be devastating for older employees (Vinokur, et al., 1991; Warr, 1987). This research suggests that unemployment is frequently associated with depression, insomnia, irritability, lack of confidence, and general anxiety.

Shaffer (1987) proposes a less consistent pattern of results between work satisfaction and life satisfaction. She argues that previous work in this field has revealed few consistent relationships between life satisfaction and job satisfaction. Her work suggests that individuals can be grouped according to the relationship between their work and nonwork satisfaction patterns are consistent over time. Using data collected on a large group of college students who completed a survey during their first year at college and again 12 to 15 years later, she found five different subgroups of men and six subgroups of women with distinct patterns of work and nonwork satisfaction. Shaffer found that most people in this study were satisfied with both their work and nonwork activities, but there were additional patterns of work and non-work satisfaction within the sample. Table 4 describes the patterns of satisfaction found in Shaffer's study.

126

Table 5
Patterns of Work and Non-Work Satisfaction Found in Shaffer (1987)

Men and Women:

Generally satisfied: High to moderate satisfaction with life and work.

Generally dissatisfied: low satisfaction with life and work

Non-work Compensators: high satisfaction with life and low satisfaction with work

Work Compensators: high work satisfaction and low life satisfaction

Materially dissatisfied: dissatisfied with both life and work environments

Women Only:

Dissatisfied Isolates: dissatisfied with work and personal relationships.

Section Summary

Job satisfaction is defined as the positive or negative evaluation that an employee makes of the work and work environment. I/O psychologists have approached job satisfaction from two angles: what are the sources of satisfaction and dissatisfaction and what are the consequences of these evaluations. Research on the sources of satisfaction have led to a number of theories including facet models of job satisfaction which describe overall satisfaction as the summary of satisfaction with specific aspects of the work and work environment. Herzberg developed a two factor theory which suggests that job satisfaction and dissatisfaction arise from different aspects of work. The job characteristics model emphasizes how specific features of the job influence job satisfaction. In contrast, recent efforts have attempted to explain the apparent stability of job satisfaction over time and have suggested that job attitudes may be at least in part an individual difference variable, some people may be more likely to be satisfied with their work than others.

Research on the consequences of job satisfaction have focused on three sets of outcomes. First, how does satisfaction or dissatisfaction affect organizational withdrawal? This research suggests that satisfaction is related to turnover, absenteeism and tardiness. Second, how do job attitudes affect productivity? Overall, this research does not support the conclusion that the happy worker is a productive worker. Finally, how does job satisfaction interact with life satisfaction? Again the results are mixed. There does not seem to be a consistent relationship between how an employee feels about work and how he or she feels about life in general.

References

Adams, J. S. (1963). Toward an understanding of inequity. *Journal of Abnormal and Social Psychology, 67,* 422-436.

Alderfer, C. P. (1969). An empirical test of a new theory of human needs. *Organizational Behavior and Human Performance, 4,* 142-175.

Arvey, R. D., Bouchard, T. J. Jr., Segal, N. L. & Abraham, L. M. (1989). Job satisfaction: Environmental and genetic components. *Journal of Applied Psychology, 74 (2),* 187-192.

Ash, P., Slora, K., & Britton, C. (1990). Police agency officer selection practices. *Journal of Police Science Administration, 17,* 258-269.

Baldwin, T. T. & Ford, J. K. (1988). Transfer of training: A review and directions for future research. *Personnel Psychology, 41,* 63-105.

Baldwin, T. T. & Magjuka, R. J. (1991). Organizational training and signals of importance: Effects of pretraining perceptions on intentions to transfer. *Human Resources Development, 2* (1), 25-36.

Bandura, A. (1982). Self-efficacy mechanism in human agency. *American Psychologist, 37,* 122-147.

Bandura, A. (1986). *Social foundations of thought and action.* Englewood Cliffs, NJ: Prentice Hall.

Barrick, M. R. & Mount, M. K. (1993). Autonomy as a moderator of the relationship between the big five personality dimensions and job performance. *Journal of Applied Psychology, 78* (1), 111-118.

Bernick, E. L., Kindley, R. & Pettit, K. K. (1984). The structure of training courses and the effects of hierarchy. *Public Personnel Management, 13,* 109-119.

Bouchard, T. J. Jr., Arvey, R. D., Keller, L. M., & Segal, N. L. (1992). Genetic influences on job satisfaction: A reply to

Cropanzano and James. *Journal of Applied Psychology, 77 (1)*, 89-93.

Brockner, J. (1990). Scope of justice in the workplace: How survivors react to co-worker layoffs. *Journal of Social Issues, 46 (1)*, 95-106.

Campbell, J. P. & Campbell, R. J. (1988). Introduction: What Industrial-Organizational psychology has to say about productivity. In J. P. Campbell and R. J. Campbell (Eds.), *Productivity in organizations: New perspectives from industrial and organizational psychology* (pp. 1-10). San Francisco: Jossey Bass.

Campbell, J. P. (1988). Training design for performance improvement. In J. P. Campbell and R. J. Campbell (Eds.), *Productivity in organizations: New perspectives from industrial and organizational psychology* (pp. 177-215). San Francisco: Jossey Bass.

Campbell, J. P. & Pritchard, R. D. (1976). Motivational theory in industrial and organizational psychology. In M. D. Dunnette (Ed.), *Handbook of industrial and organizational psychology*. Chicago: Rand McNally.

Campion, M. A. (1991). Meaning and measurement of turnover: Comparison of alternative measures and recommendations for research. *Journal of Applied Psychology, 76 (2)*, 199-212.

Carnevale, A. P., Gainer, L. J., & Villet, J. (1990). *Training in America: The organization and strategic role of training.* San Francisco: Jossey Bass.

Cascio, W. F. (1991). *Applied psychology in personnel management.* Englewood Cliffs, N.J.: Prentice Hall.

Cassidy-Schmitt, M. C. & Newby, T. J. (1986). Metacognition: Relevance to instructional design. *Journal of Instructional Development, 9,* 20-33.

Cherrington, D. J. (1989). Need theories of motivation. In R. M. Steers and L. W. Porter (Eds.), *Motivation and work behavior* (pp. 31-43). New York: McGraw Hill

Cohen, D. J. (1990). What motivates trainees. *Training and Development Journal*, Nov., 91-93.

Digman, J. M. (1990). Personality structure: Emergence of the five factor model. *Annual Review of Psychology* (Vol. 41, pp. 417-440). Palo Alto, CA: Annual reviews.

Doran,, L. I., Stone, V. K., Brief, A. P. & George, J. M. (1991). Behavioral intentions as predictors of job attitudes: The role of economic choice. *Journal of Applied Psychology, 76*, 40-45.

Dunnette, M. D. (1990). Blending the science and practice of industrial and organizational psychology: Where are we and where are we going. In M. D. Dunnette and L. M. Hough (Eds.), *Handbook of industrial and organizational psychology* (2nd ed., Vol.. 1, pp. 1-28). Palo Alto, CA: Consulting Psychologists Press.

Fiedler, F. E. (1989). The effective utilization of intellectual abilities and job-relevant knowledge in group performance: cognitive resource theory and an agenda for the future. *Applied Psychology: An International Review, 38*, 289-304.

Gerhart, B. (1990). Voluntary turnover and alternative job opportunities. *Journal of Applied Psychology, 75 (5)*, 467-476.

Gibson, F. W., Fiedler, F. E., & Daniels, K. M. (1990). Determinants of effective utilization of leader abilities: Stress, babble, and the utilization of leader intellectual abilities. (Tech. Rep. No. 90-1), University of Washington, Seattle.

Gist, M. E., Schoerer, C. & Rosen, B. (1989). Effects of alternative training methods on self-efficacy and performance in computer software training. *Journal of Applied Psychology, 74*, 884-891.

Goldberg, L. R. (1990). An alternative "description of personality": The Big-Five factor structure. *Journal of Personality and Social Psychology, 59*, 1216-1229.

Goldstein, I. L. (1986). *Training in organizations: Needs assessment, development, and evaluation.* Monterey, CA: Brooks/Cole.

Goldstein, I. L. & Gilliam, P. (1990). Training issues in the year 2000. *American Psychologist, 45 (2),* 134-143.

Greenberg, J. (1990). Employee theft as a reaction to underpayment inequity: The hidden cost of pay cuts. *Journal of Applied Psychology, 75 (5),* 561-568.

Guilford, J. S., Zimmerman, W., & Guilford, J. P. (1976). *The Guilford-Zimmerman Temperament Survey handbook.* Palo Alto, CA: Consulting Psychologists Press.

Guion, R.M. (1991) Personnel assessment, selection, and placement. In M. D. Dunnette and L. M. Hough (Eds.), *Handbook of industrial and organizational psychology* (2nd ed., Vol.. 2, pp. 327-398). Palo Alto, CA: Consulting Psychologists Press.

Hackman, J. R. & Oldham, G. R. (1976). Motivation through the design of work: Test of a theory. *Organizational Behavior and Human Performance, 16,* 250-279.

Hakel, M. D. (1982). Employment interviewing. In K. M. Rowland & G. R. Ferris (Eds.), *Personnel management.* Boston: Allyn & Bacon.

Hakel, M. D. (1986). Personnel selection and placement. *Annual Review of Psychology,* (Vol.. 37, pp. 351-380). Palo Alto, CA: Annual Reviews.

Hall , D. T. & Nougaim, K. E. (1968). An examination of Maslow's need hierarchy in an organizational setting. *Organizational Behavior and Human Performance, 3,* 12-35.

Harder, J. W. (1991). Equity theory versus expectancy theory: The case of major league baseball free agents. *Journal of Applied Psychology, 76* (3), 458-464.

Harvey, (1991). Job Analysis. In M. D. Dunnette and L. M. Hough (Eds.), *Handbook of industrial and organizational psychology*, (2nd ed., Vol.. 2, pp. 71- 163). Palo Alto, CA: Consulting Psychologists Press.

Harvey, R. J., Friedman, L., Hakel, M. D., & Cornelius, E. T. (1988). Dimensionality of the Job Element Inventory, a simplified worker oriented job analysis questionnaire. *Journal of Applied Psychology, 73,* 639-646.

Heilman, M. E., Block, C. J., & Lucas, J. A. (1992). Presumed incompetent? Stigmatization and affirmative action efforts. *Journal of Applied Psychology, 77,* 536-544.

Herriot, P. (1989). Selection as a social process. In M. Smith and I. T. Robertson, (Eds.), *Advances in selection and assessment.* Chichester, England: Wiley.

Herzberg, F. (1968). One more time: How do you motivate employees? *Harvard Business Review, 46,* 53-62.

Hogan, R. T. (1991). Personality and personality measurement. In M. D. Dunnette and L. M. Hough (Eds.), *Handbook of industrial and organizational psychology.* (2nd ed., Vol.. 2, pp. 873-919). Palo Alto, CA: Consulting Psychologists Press.

Hogan, P. M., Hakel, M. D., & Decker, P. J. (1986). Effects of trainee-generated versus trainer-provided rule codes on generalization in behavior-modeling training. *Journal of Applied Psychology, 71,* 469-473.

Hough, L. M., Eaton, N. K., Dunnette, M. D., Kamp, J. D., & McCloy, R. A. (1990). Criterion-related validities of personality constructs and the effect of response distortion on those validities. *Journal of Applied Psychology Monograph, 75,* 581-595.

Howard, A. (1991). Industrial/Organizational Psychologists as practitioners. In D. W. Bray (Ed.) *Working with organizations and their people: A guide for human resource practitioners* (pp. 13-44). New York: Guilford Press.

Hulin, C. (1991). Adaptation, persistence and commitment in organizations. In M. D. Dunnette and L. M. Hough (Eds.), *Handbook of industrial and organizational psychology* (2nd ed., Vol.. 2, pp. 445-506). Palo Alto, CA: Consulting Psychologists Press.

James, L. A. & James, L. R. (1989). Integrating work environment perceptions: Explorations into the measurement of meaning. *Journal of Applied Psychology, 74 (5),* 739-751.

James, L. R. & Tetrick, L. E. (1986). Confirmatory factor analytic tests of three causal models relating job perceptions to job satisfaction. *Journal of Applied Psychology, 71,* 77-82.

Kanfer, R. (1990). Motivation theory and industrial and organizational psychology. In M. D. Dunnette and L. M. Hough (Eds.), *Handbook of industrial and organizational psychology* (2nd ed., Vol.. 1, pp. 75-170). Palo Alto, CA: Consulting Psychologists Press.

Katzell, R. A. & Thompson, D. E. (1990). Work motivation: Theory and practice. *American Psychologist, 45* (2), 144-153.

Katzell, R. A. & Austin, J. T. (1992) From then to now: The development of industrial-organizational psychology in the United States. *Journal of Applied Psychology, 77,* 803-835.

Keller, L. M., Bouchard, T. J. Jr., Arvey, R. D., Segal, N. L. & Dawis, R. V. (1992).Work values: Genetic and environmental influences. *Journal of Applied Psychology, 77,* 79-88.

Kerr, S. (1987). On the folly of rewarding A, while hoping for B. In R.M. Steers and L.W. Porter (Eds.), *Motivation and work behavior* (pp. 485-498). New York: McGraw Hill

Kirkpatrick, D. L. (1976). Evaluation of training. In R.L. Craig (Ed.), *Training and Development Handbook* (pp. 18-1 - 18-27). New York: McGraw Hill.

Komaki, J. L., Coombs, T., & Schepman, S. (1991). Motivational implications of reinforcement theory. In R. M. Steers and L. W. Porter (Eds.), *Motivation and work behavior* (pp. 87-107). New York: McGraw Hill

Lahiri, D. K., & Srivastva, S. (1967). Determinants of satisfaction in middle management personnel. *Journal of Applied Psychology, 51,* 254-265.

Latham, G. P. (1988). Human resource training and development. *Annual Review of Psychology, 39,* 545-582.

Latham, G. P. & Saari, L. M. (1984). Do people do what they say? Further studies on the situational interview. *Journal of Applied Psychology, 69,* 569-573.

Lawler, E. E. (1987). Pay for performance: A motivational analysis. In H.R. Nalbatian (Ed.), *Incentives, cooperation and risk sharing.* Totowa, NJ: Rowman & Littlefield.

Lawler, E. E. (1973). *Motivation in work organizations.* Monterey, CA: Brooks/Cole Publishing.

Lawler, E. E. & Suttle, J. L. (1972). A causal correlational test of the need hierarchy concept. *Organizational Behavior and Human Performance, 7,* 265-287.

Locke, E. A. (1968). Toward a task theory of motivation and incentives. *Organizational Behavior and Human Performance, 3,* 157-189.

Locke, E. A. (1976). The nature and causes of job satisfaction. In M. D. Dunnette (Ed.), *The handbook of industrial and organizational psychology.* Chicago: Rand McNally.

Locke, E. A., Shaw, K. N., Saari, L. M., & Latham, G. P. (1981). Goal setting and task performance: 1969-1980. *Psychological Bulletin, 90,* 125-152.

Mahoney, T. A. (1988). Productivity defined: The relativity of efficiency, effectiveness and change. In J. P. Campbell and R. J. Campbell (Eds.), *Productivity in organizations: New perspectives from industrial and organizational psychology* (pp. 13-39). San Francisco: Jossey Bass.

Maslow, A. H. (1943). A theory of motivation. *Psychological Review, 50,* 370-396.

McClelland, D. C. (1987). *Human motivation.* New York: Cambridge University Press.

McClelland, D. C. & Boyatzis, R. E. (1982). The leadership motive pattern and long term success in management. *Journal of Applied Psychology, 67 (6),* 737-743.

McCormick, E. J., Jeanneret, P., & Mecham, R. C. (1972). A study of job characteristics of job dimensions as based on the position analysis questionnaire, *Journal of Applied Psychology Monograph, 36,* 347-368.

McHenry, J. J., Hough, L. M., Toquam, J. L., Hanson, M. A., & Ashworth, S. (1990). Project A validity results: The relationship between predictor and criterion domains. *Personnel Psychology, 43* (2), 335-354.

Mecham, R. C., McCormick, E. J., & Jeanneret, P. R. (1977). *Position analysis questionnaire: User's manual, System II.* West Lafayette, IN: PAQ Services.

Meglino, B. M., DeNisi, A. S., Youngblood, S. A. & Williams, K. J. (1988). Effects of realistic job previews: A comparison using an enhancement and a reduction preview. *Journal of Applied Psychology, 73,* 259-266.

Mitchell, T. R. (1974). Expectancy models of job satisfaction, occupational preference, and effort: A theoretical, methodological, and empirical approach. *Psychological Bulletin, 81,* 1053-1077.

Mitchell, T. R. and Silver, W. S. (1990). Individual and group goals when workers are interdependent: Effects on task strategies and performance. *Journal of Applied Psychology, 75* (2), 185-193.

Mobley, W. H. (1977). Intermediate linkages in the relationship between job satisfaction and employee turnover. *Journal of Applied Psychology, 62,* 237-240.

Mobley, W. H., Horner, S. O., & Hollingsworth, A. T. (1978). An evaluation of precursors of hospital employee turnover. *Journal of Applied Psychology, 63,* 408-414.

Motowidlo, S. J., Carter, G. W., Dunnette, M. D., Tippens, N., Werner, S. Burnett, J. R., & Vaughan, M. J. (1992). Studies of the structured behavioral interview. *Journal of Applied Psychology, 77,* 571-587.

Murphy, S. E., Blythe, D., & Fiedler, F. E. (1990). Cognitive resource theory and the utilization of the leader's and group members technical competence. (Tech. Rep. No. 90-2). University of Washington, Seattle.

Noe, R. A. (1986). Trainees' attributes and attitudes: Neglected influences on training effectiveness. *Academy of Management Review, 11,* 736-749.

Noe, R. A. (1988). An investigation of the determinants of successfully assigned mentoring relationships. *Personnel Psychology, 41,* 457-479.

Normand, J., Salyards, S. D., & Mahoney, J. J. (1990). An evaluation of pre-employment drug testing. *Journal of Applied Psychology, 75 (6),* 629-639.

O'Reilly, C. A. (1991). Organizational behavior: Where we've been, where we're going. *Annual Review of Psychology, 42,* 427-458.

Petty, M. M., Singleton, B., & Connell, D. W. (1992). An experimental evaluation of an organizational incentive plan in the electric utility industry. *Journal of Applied Psychology, 77 (4),* 427-436.

Porter, L. W., & Lawler, E. E. (1968). *Managerial attitudes and performance.* Homewood, IL: Dorsey

Pritchard, R. D., Roth, P. L., Jones, S. D., Galgay, P. J., & Watson, M. D.(1988). Designing a goal-setting system to enhance performance: A practical guide. *Organizational Dynamics, 17,* 69-78.

Rice, R. W., Gentile, D. A. & McFarlin, D. B. (1991). Facet importance and job satisfaction. *Journal of Applied Psychology, 76 (1),* 31-39.

Rodgers, R. and Hunter, J. E. (1991). Impact of management by objectives on organizational productivity. *Journal of Applied Psychology, 76 (2),* 322-336.

137

Rynes, S. L. (1991). Recruitment, job choice, and post-hire consequences: A call for new research directions. In M. D. Dunnette and L. M. Hough (Eds.), *Handbook of industrial and organizational psychology.* (2nd ed., Vol.. 2, pp. 399-444). Palo Alto, CA: Consulting Psychologists Press.

Saal, F. E. & Moore, S. C. (1993). Perceptions of promotion fairness and promotion candidates' qualifications. *Journal of Applied Psychology, 78,* 105-110.

Schmidt, F. L., Ones, D. S., & Hunter, J. E. (1992). Personnel selection. *Annual Review of Psychology* (Vol.. 43, pp. 627-670). Palo Alto, CA: Annual Reviews.

Schmitt, N. (1976). Social and situational determinants of interview decisions: Implications for the employment interview. *Personnel Psychology, 29,*79-101.

Shaffer, G. S. (1987). Patterns of work and nonwork satisfaction. *Journal of Applied Psychology, 72 (1),* 115-124.

Snow, R. E. & Lohman, D. F. (1984). Toward a theory of cognitive aptitude for learning and instruction. *Journal of Educational Psychology, 76,* 347-376.

Specter, P. E. & Jex, S. M. (1991). Relations of job characteristics from multiple data sources with employee affect, absence, turnover intentions and health. *Journal of Applied Psychology, 76 (1),* 46-53.

Staw, B. M. (1991). Organizational psychology and the pursuit of the happy/productive worker. In R. M. Steers and L. W. Porter, (Eds.), *Motivation and work behavior* (pp. 264-276). New York: McGraw Hill.

Staw, B. M. & Ross, J. (1985). Stability in the midst of change: A dispositional approach to job attitudes. *Journal of Applied Psychology, 70,* 469-480.

Sterns, H. L. & Doverspike, D. (1989). Aging and the training and learning process in organizations. In I. L. Goldstein (Ed.), *Training and development in work organizations: Frontiers of industrial and organizational psychology* (pp. 121-182). San Francisco: Jossey Bass.

Tannenbaum, S. & Yukl, G. (1992). Training and development in work organizations. *Annual Review of Psychology, 43,* 399-442.

Tosi, H. & Tosi, L. (1986). What managers need to know about knowledge-based pay. *Organizational Dynamics, 14,* 52-64.

Tucker, F. D. (1985). A study of the training needs of older workers: Implications for human resources development planning. *Public Personnel Management, 14,* 85-95.

Ulrich, L. & Trumbo, D. (1965). The selection interview since 1949. *Psychological Bulletin, 63,* 100-116.

Vinokur, A. D., van Ryn, M., Gramlich, E. M., and Price, R. H. (1991). Long-term follow-up and benefit cost analysis of the jobs program: A preventative intervention for the unemployed. *Journal of Applied Psychology, 76 (2),* 213-220.

Wanous, J. P. (1977). Organizational entry: Newcomers moving from outside to inside. *Psychological Bulletin, 84,* 601-618.

Wanous, J. P. & Zwany, A. (1977). A cross-sectional test of need-hierarchy theory. *Organizational Behavior and Human Performance, 18,* 78-79.

Warr, P. B. (1987). *Work, unemployment and mental health.* Oxford: Clarendon Press.

Winefield, A. H., Winefield, H. R., Tiggemann, M., & Goldney, R. D. (1991). A longitudinal study of the psychological effects of unemployment and unsatisfactory employment on young adults. *Journal of Applied Psychology, 76 (3),* 424-431.

Notes

Notes

Notes

Notes

Notes

Notes